MEASURING UP

*An Oral History
of*
Harvey Picker

Edited by
Carolyn Marsh

A BRANTA BOOK

Copyright ©2012 by Branta Books

All rights reserved. Except for brief passages quoted in a newspaper, magazine, radio or television review, no part of this nook may be reproduced in any form or by any means, electronic or mechanical, including photocopying and recording, or by any information storage and retrieval system, without permission in writing from the Publisher.

A Branta Book
in association with Epigraph Publishing
P.O. Box 533
Somers, N.Y. 10589

ISBN 978-1-936940-28-8
Library of Congress Control Number: 2012936695

Designed by Elizabeth DiPalma

Printed in the United States of America

I am part of all that I have met.

— FROM "ULYSSES," BY ALFRED, LORD TENNYSON

Contents

Foreword   ix

3	CHAPTER 1	Picker X-Ray: The Early Days
12	CHAPTER 2	Childhood
19	CHAPTER 3	Higher Education
27	CHAPTER 4	Rowing
35	CHAPTER 5	A Company Man
41	CHAPTER 6	The Navy
46	CHAPTER 7	The Rad Lab
52	CHAPTER 8	Developing Picker X-Ray
61	CHAPTER 9	Jean
70	CHAPTER 10	Aloft
72	CHAPTER 11	Picker and CIT
75	CHAPTER 12	The Hudson Institute
78	CHAPTER 13	A Student Again
82	CHAPTER 14	Jean: Her Life
86	CHAPTER 15	Jean and I
91	CHAPTER 16	Travels Together
102	CHAPTER 17	In the Soviet Union

109	Chapter 18	Teaching at Colgate
113	Chapter 19	Graduate School of International Affairs
123	Chapter 20	Philanthropy
130	Chapter 21	Politics
132	Chapter 22	Wayfarer and Camden
143	Chapter 23	Life in Maine
		151 *Camden Public Library*
		154 *Mid-Coast Forum on Foreign Relations*
		155 *The Camden Conference*
157	Chapter 24	The James Picker Foundation
160	Chapter 25	The American Way of Dying
165	Chapter 26	The Picker Surveys
172	Chapter 27	Picker Institute
175	Chapter 28	The Future of Healthcare in This Country
179		A Short Biography of Harvey Picker

Foreword

Harvey Picker was born on Dec. 8, 1915, in New York City. He died on March 22, 2008, in Camden, Maine. In those 92 years he made his mark as a physicist, an inventor, an educator, a businessman and a philanthropist, and throughout his life he took on many other roles that are not so easy to define. He adored his wife, Jean, who was his partner in everything he did; and he loved his daughters, Bobbi and Gale, his grandchildren and his many, many friends.

Harvey graduated from Colgate University in 1936 and from Harvard Business School with an MBA in 1938. He also studied at Oxford University for a year, and his memories of that time range from his experience as a member of an Oxford eight to his misgivings about Hitler and the renascence of Germany, dark shadows over those golden days.

In 1938 Harvey joined Picker X-Ray Company, which his father, James Picker, had founded two decades earlier. When war broke out in Europe, Picker X-Ray, in collaboration with the U.S. Army, transformed battlefield medicine with the development of field X-ray equipment small enough to fit into a trio of footlockers and sturdy enough to be dropped by parachute to wherever it was needed. At the end of the war, Harvey and his father sent the U.S. Treasury a check for $4 million, representing the company's profits from those field X-ray machines, with a letter explaining that the family did not wish to profit from the war effort. The gesture was something the government had never seen before.

While in the Navy, Harvey was chosen to work on the secret development of radar with a team of physicists at the Radiation Laboratory at MIT in Cambridge, Mass. At the Rad Lab, as it was known, he felt like a kid in a candy store, and his recounting of his adventures there is as bright as his future was to be.

After returning to civilian life, Harvey headed Picker X-Ray Company for 25 years, leading the company into such new fields as cobalt therapy for cancer, nuclear imaging diagnostics and the use of ultrasound for oceanography, which was then adapted for medical imaging.

In 1971, Harvey returned to his alma mater, Colgate University, as an adjunct faculty member. Among the courses he taught were "Social Control of Science and Technology" and "The Politics of Assassination." He loved teaching, and his classes were regularly booked to the limit.

In 1972, Harvey was asked to serve as dean of the Columbia University School of International and Public Affairs at Columbia, despite the fact that he had neither an advanced degree nor any professional experience in the field of international relations. During his tenure, the students at the school tripled in number, not least because he focused the school on teaching the skills needed to perform jobs crucial to international industry as well as politics.

Jean Picker, who served as an ambassador to the United Nations in the 1960s, was an active collaborator in all of her husband's interests. She died in 1990.

Harvey and Jean were both avid sailors. In 1982 they moved to Camden, Maine, and Harvey bought and ran Wayfarer Marine Corp., one of the largest boatyards on the East Coast with an international reputation for quality craftsmanship.

In keeping with his commitment to public service, Harvey served on many boards throughout his lifetime, among them the New York Philharmonic, Hudson Institute, Colgate University, Lenox Hill Hospital, New Rochelle Hospital and the Radiological Society Research and Education Foundation. He was a member of the National Science Board and of the International Atomic Energy Agency.

As a resident of Camden he served on many local and state boards, including the Maine Health Care Finance Commission, the Blue-Ribbon Commission to Overhaul the Workers' Compensation Insurance System and the Camden Public Library.

In 1994 Harvey took over the operations of Picker Institute, which he had founded with his wife in 1987. A global independent nonprofit organization, Picker Institute is dedicated to advancing healthcare as seen "through the patient's eyes."

The institute, which is credited with having coined the phrase "patient-centered care," pioneered patient-satisfaction surveys for the systematic collection of data from hospital patients to help improve the delivery of medical services. The Picker Surveys have become a standard measure of patient care worldwide.

In 1999 Harvey founded the Picker Engineering Program at Smith College, his wife's alma mater. The first engineering program at a women's college, it has become a model for attracting women to engineering.

Harvey always relished the challenge of, and took great pleasure in, finding ways to empower people through education, a belief that he applied fully and fruitfully to his own life. He was a reliable and generous friend to many. He believed that identifying problems and solving them was the most fun a person could have other than sailing along the Maine coast on a sunny September afternoon.

Harvey was a painfully modest man. He agreed to record his recollections when he was close to 90 years old, and then only at the insistence of his close friend and lawyer, Christine Beshar. He never finished the recordings, nor did he take the time to review the transcripts, but he asked me to edit what was there. Some of these chapters, therefore, remain incomplete and fragmentary.

>Carolyn Marsh
>Camden, Maine
>February 2012

Measuring Up

[1]
Picker X-Ray: The Early Days

My father, James Picker, emigrated from Russia to the United States in 1890. He came alone, and when he got off the ship in New York, even though he didn't know any English, he said, "I'm never going to speak Russian again."

He learned English and got a job as a delivery boy in a pharmacy in New York City. He also started to study pharmacology. His employer let him sleep in a room at the back of the pharmacy so he could be available for emergency deliveries. My father annoyed his employer by continuing to study.

My father not only earned a pharmacy degree but ended up owning the pharmacy. It was on 99th Street, next to Mt. Sinai Hospital. Because it was so close to the hospital and many of his customers were doctors and nurses, my father expanded from what was customary in those days, which was just filling prescriptions. He added a soda fountain as well as such items as Brownie cameras and Kodak film.

In 1915, the year I was born, my father moved from the pharmacy field into X-ray supplies and equipment. I was told this is why he made the change: One day he heard the nurses at the soda fountain talking about a strange new device next to the coal bin in the hospital basement. It was called a Roentgen ray machine. In 1895, Wilhelm Conrad Roentgen had discovered a previously unknown radiation, which he called X-rays because neither he nor anyone else knew anything about it at that time.

The nurses were talking about how difficult it was for Mt. Sinai's roentgenologist, Dr. Jackes, to get the X-ray plates he needed to record the images he had obtained. In those days, X-ray film didn't exist. Instead, big glass plates coated with silver were used. The plates were so heavy that they could be moved only about a dozen at a time, in wooden crates, very much as a piano would be. These X-ray plates were made by Kodak, and my father had the agency for Kodak's small, inexpensive Brownie camera.

James Picker went to the basement of Mt. Sinai Hospital to talk to Dr. Jackes about the problem. The doctor told my father he was having great trouble getting X-ray plates from Kodak. When my father asked whether he could supply the hospital with these plates, Dr. Jackes was delighted.

Dr. Jackes had found Kodak very difficult to deal with, and it turned out that Kodak was more than glad to rid itself of having to make sure that plates were not mishandled and were delivered on time.

My father started selling X-ray plates. He found the work interesting and remunerative. Over time his business expanded to include most New York hospitals, and later hospitals in Boston, Philadelphia and, surprisingly, New Orleans. Then, since he was selling the plates, he began to sell some of the accessories that were needed when using Roentgen-ray machines.

This business was so good that my father sold the pharmacy shortly thereafter, along with the medical supplies business he had developed, and formed the James Picker Co. to provide radiologists with supplies for X-ray machines. (We now call them radiologists instead of roentgenologists.) The company prospered, and my father obtained an agency to sell X-ray machines made by a company called Acme.

In the early days of X-ray manufacturing, as in the early days of automobile manufacturing, there were about 80 or 90 X-ray machine manufacturers. Acme was one of them. Their machines had enough advantages over other machines so that the James Picker Co. gained a small but noticeable part of the market. In 1921 the name of the company was changed to Picker X-Ray Corp.

Then General Electric became interested in the field and bought out one of Acme's competitors, Victoreen. That move by General Electric led its major competitor, Westinghouse, to decide that it ought to follow suit. Westinghouse bought Acme. My father received notice that in something like 60 or 90 days, he would no longer have the Acme agency and that Westinghouse was going to deal with the radiologists directly. That left my father without what had become over the past several years an important part of his business. In 1929 he began to search for a company to supply X-ray machines. He found it very difficult to find one that he thought was outstanding, but he finally discovered a company, Waite & Bartlett, in Long Island City, New York. Waite & Bartlett held all the patents on how to manufacture "shock-proof" X-ray machines.

Even though the significant long-term dangers from radiation were not known in those days, everyone understood the obvious danger to doctors, patients and nurses of electrocution from the very high voltages—close to 100,000 volts—needed to operate the X-ray tube. Anyone coming near the electrical wires leading to the X-ray tube could be killed instantly. This danger was made all the greater because many types of illnesses had to be examined in pitch-dark rooms. As one would expect, there was a small but appreciable immediate death toll from X-ray examinations.

By the mid-1920s, Waite & Bartlett had devised and patented the only three ways to completely safeguard X-ray examinations against electrical shock. All the dental machines you see today were originally invented and patented by Waite & Bartlett. The company also held patents on two other kinds of shock-proof X-ray machines. Picker X-Ray bought the Waite & Bartlett company.

As it turned out, Waite & Bartlett had great ingenuity but was not a good manufacturer. Around 1930, my father decided he wanted to produce better, higher-quality machines. He searched around for somebody to take over the manufacturing and found a man at the head of one of the competitive organizations, Ed Goldfield, in Cleveland, Ohio. Ed had been warned that James Picker was a very difficult person to deal with, but he and my father hit it off so well that my father decided the Waite & Bartlett machines ought to be built under Goldfield's direction. Goldfield had no desire to move to New York. In fact, he insisted that he was going to stay in Cleveland, because at that time Cleveland was one of the major manufacturing centers for automobiles and therefore a good source for workers who had the kinds of skills to make the mechanical parts of X-ray machines. You couldn't get such workers around New York, so my father decided to move the factory from Long Island City to Cleveland.

This was just about when the Great Depression started. Ed Goldfield had decided that equipment shouldn't be built the way it was, with special pieces for each type of machine. He believed the most efficient thing to do was build common parts so all machines used absolutely identical parts, whether it was one kind of machine or another. Despite the need for income, Goldfield was taking a long time to design and build these parts. The result was that my father's investment produced no machines year after year, and this was during the Depression.

A Picker X-Ray sales meeting in Cleveland. Harvey, wearing a white shirt and a dark tie, sits in the middle of the front row.

There was no Social Security program at this time. People who lost their job lost their ability even to obtain food unless they went to a soup kitchen. My father called the employees of Picker X-Ray together—I think this is a very interesting contrast to today—and he said, "I'm not sure how well we're going to be able to last through this, but I can tell you this: Your job is safe here until the entire company goes broke." It was typical of his thinking.

This instilled in me the belief that good, skilled workers were more important than the stockholders, and therefore their job security was more important than the stockholders' security (even though my father was the sole stockholder).

In the 1920s, X-ray machines began using a red film base instead of the big glass plates. Film was much easier and cheaper to use, and Kodak was the only supplier in the United States of any size. The film itself had a nitrate base, so while it looked like present-day film, it was very flammable.

There were many deaths from stored X-ray films that caught fire. Even if the fires didn't kill people outright, many died because the fumes from the burning nitrate were highly toxic.

One of the worst fires was in 1929 in the X-ray film storage unit at the Crile Clinic in Cleveland (now the Cleveland Hospital), which killed a large number of patients, nurses and doctors.

My father learned that Pathé, in France, was making an acetate-based film, which, while it could burn, didn't burn readily and didn't give off poisonous fumes if it did. By this time, Picker was by far the largest purchaser of Kodak X-ray film. My father had asked Kodak to change from a nitrate- to an acetate-based film, but Kodak said that process would take at least three or four years. So my father sent a telegraphic order to Pathé for a large amount of acetate-based film, and sent a copy of the order to Kodak.

When the Pathé film arrived in the United States, my father took it around to the various hospitals himself, instead of having a salesman do it, and explained the difference to the hospitals. Pathé film was really not quite as good for diagnostic purposes as the Kodak film, he said, but they should use it because it was safer for everybody in the hospital.

The result was a large drop-off in orders to Kodak. When this happened, Kodak, instead of taking several years, decided it could produce acetate-based film a lot faster. And in less than a year Kodak came out with an acetate-based film that was better than Pathé's product.

My father went to each of the hospitals that he had convinced to use the Pathé film and exchanged the remaining Pathé film for the better Kodak. He absorbed the loss of the Pathé film, which he took back and threw away.

The idea that you did the best you could for the customer and not for your profit was an essential part of my education.

As a pharmacist, my father was always looking for improvements, and one of the dubious delights of being his son was being used as a guinea pig. When the family moved to New Rochelle, the house had a pool room for billiards and other games. There was a little bathroom off of it, which my father used as an experiment room. I'd walk by the bathroom and a hand would pop out with a glass and the command, "Drink this and tell me how it tastes."

Harvey in his early teens, around the time he was acting as a guinea pig for his father.

With his experience in X-ray technology, my father knew a lot about the various substances given to patients in order to visualize body parts. For example, in order to view the digestive tract, patients had to swallow barium sulfate.

We still use barium sulfate today, but in those days barium sulfate had the consistency of sand and tasted terrible. The poor person who was having his gastrointestinal tract examined had to try and gulp the stuff down before it settled at the bottom of the glass. My father had the good idea, now widely used, of adding a suspension and a flavoring agent. He fed it to me first. Eventually it was sold under the trade name of Basolac and turned out to be a fairly profitable business.

If you wanted to visualize the gall bladder, you had to give people something, as you do today, that has a high iodine content but is not poisonous. In those days a chemical named sodium tetraiodophenolphthalein was used. It worked fine, except that if it was exposed to air for any length of time, it became profoundly irritating to the stomach. So a person going in for a gall bladder examination was treated to something that acted as, from time to time, an emetic, and the stomach would react violently. To eliminate that, my father put the sodium tetraiodophenolphthalein into an enteric-coated capsule that dissolved in the intestine, not in the stomach. It was called Kerasol, and it became quite popular. But you had to take quite a few big pills that were difficult to swallow, so my father tried to find a way of making something that was a powder that could be dissolved in a safe and palatable drink.

My father eventually held the patent on a number of other things, such as lead rubber gloves. When I was a boy, a good number of radiologists who'd been in business for a while had lost some of their fingers. Many of them had died from exposure to X-rays, because at first they didn't know the danger of putting their hand in front of an X-ray. The lead rubber gloves offered quite a bit of protection, but it was hard to make a glove that was flexible and at the same time had enough lead content to protect the hand. My father had a patent on a type of glove that met both needs.

Radiology was still in its infancy—it still is, to some extent—and the field expanded very rapidly. Radiology began with X-ray machines used only for skin therapy or diagnosis. Then it expanded into treating tumors. Now medical imaging has exploded into all kinds of diagnostic equipment, including ultrasound, nuclear instrumentation for detecting and locating tumors and a whole group of other devices, including CAT scanners and

MRIs. It's a field that has grown so rapidly that now it encompasses completely different medical specialties. The genesis for everything was the original X-rays that were developed in Germany in the 1890s.

My father was an early leader in the field, and very innovative. All these advances—the X-ray equipment itself and all the allied substances and devices—were for the benefit of the patient and the doctor. This was the essence of Picker X-Ray.

[2]
Childhood

I was born Dec. 8, 1915, in New York City in a place that doesn't exist any more, a lying-in hospital. I have no idea where it was, but in those days, unless there were complications, deliveries were not normally done in acute care hospitals but in one of these very small lying-in hospitals. They were more like a converted home than an institution.

My father and mother were living in an apartment on Madison Avenue. My father's drugstore was across the street. One of my earliest memories, or perhaps fantasies, is seeing troops returning from World War I. I'd been allowed to stand on the kitchen table to crank the coffee grinder, and I "saw" soldiers marching up Fifth Avenue, which was lined with cheering citizens. The soldiers must have been among the first troops returning from World War I.

We moved to New Rochelle, New York, in the early 1920s, and I went to the public school there. However, most of my early education came from my mother, Evelyn Feil Picker. She was extremely bright. Her family had come from Poland in the early days before World War I. Her father had opened a drygoods store in West New York, a part of New Jersey at that time, but the store burned down. I often wondered whether it was because the community didn't want any damn Poles living there.

Since my grandfather Feil was having such a hard time getting on, my mother and her two brothers went to work as early as they could—and that was pretty young in those days, since there were no child labor laws. Soon, however, my mother got into Hunter College Normal School, where she did quite well.

There were two professions open to a woman in those days, nursing and teaching; my mother became a teacher. She was a very industrious, hard-working woman, and a very loving mother. She worked in the company with my father as soon as they got married, and I guess she and he were almost the entire company in those early days.

In 1909, my sister, Myrtle, was born. Myrtle became a pediatrician, a very good one. She was one of the first women to study medicine, at Columbia College of Physicians and Surgeons. She was absolutely stricken in the beginning of her second year of medicine when she began a required course on surgery. On the first day the professor looked at her and said, "I'm going to fail you." She asked, "Why? You haven't even seen my work." "Because women have no place in medicine," he replied. "You're taking the place of a man who could make this his career. Being a woman, you're going to end up having a family and just being a waste."

Somehow or other, she got through and passed the course, but this attitude was typical of an awful lot of doctors at that time.

In 1915, when I came along, the problem was how to take care of the second child. As a result of the education my mother gave me (family dinner each night was really an education in itself), I knew how to read and write well above the level of the first few grades before I went to elementary school. I had also developed a tremendous appreciation of music. I learned much, much more from my mother than I ever did in elementary school.

Nonetheless, school was a good experience. My mother insisted that I memorize great long poems or speeches such as "Spartacus to the Gladiators" or "Lepanto" and be able to declaim clearly and effectively to audiences. Somehow she communicated to my teachers that I'd memorized these pieces. So as a third-grader I'd often be asked by my teacher to stand in front of the class and recite these speeches or poems.

When I was through with my class, I was sent around to other classes, where I'd stand up in front of a group of eighth-graders—grown-up people!—and recite these poems. This was very impressive for me. It was only later that I realized that my mother had rigged the whole thing. She and my father had gotten together with my teachers and decided on this course of action to bolster my confidence. However strange it was, it gave me an ease of speaking publicly that has stood me in very good stead in all the things I've done in my life, political or academic or business.

In those days, there weren't any school buses, so I walked for 45 minutes to get to school. Nor was there any lunch at school, so I had to walk home for lunch, and walk to school again in the afternoon and then walk home.

Eventually I was sent off to a private school in Greenwich, where I was very unhappy. Then I went to the Fieldston School, in New York City, and commuted each day with four other people. I graduated from Fieldston in about 1932.

My mother was very active in the politics of New Rochelle. The town government had become very corrupt, and my mother led a crusade in town meetings that was something of a novelty

Harvey with his father, James Picker, and his sister, Myrtle (above); Myrtle (with Harvey, below) was a strong influence and support in his life.

at the time. It succeeded in reforming town government, and my mother became a local celebrity.

Along with being involved in many town activities, my mother was also a leader of the Ethical Culture movement and the head of the Sunday school organization in Westchester County. I don't need to point out that therefore I went to Sunday school every Sunday.

But what my mother did with her life exerted a profound influence on my education and my expectations of what I was going to do. She very much wanted to see me be a professor—but, alas, that didn't happen until it was too late for her to know.

My sister, Myrtle, was actually part mother and part sister to me, someone I tormented and someone who helped me in many ways, including defending me very effectively from the bullies on my way to and from school.

I got my first sailboat when I was about eight years old. I was lying on the floor one rainy Sunday reading the comics, and my father walked in and said, "How would you like to have a sailboat?"

I think this was prompted by the fact that some friends of ours had invited us to go sailing during the summer. I was so enthralled by it that they invited us out again. I must have communicated my pleasure quite clearly to my parents. So with my mother's encouragement, my father had gone out and bought me a sailboat.

I reacted exactly as you would if someone walked into the room and said, "Do you want a hundred million dollars?" You'd say, "Sure," and you'd go on with what you're doing. My sister, who'd come in with my father, said, "No, really. You've got a little green boat and it's got sails. Come look at it."

I fell in love with sailing on the spot. I don't know where this love came from, but I'm still happy just sitting on a boat at the mooring. I enjoy the quiet feeling of waves under the boat and the intricacies of navigating.

CHILDHOOD 17

Harvey at the wheel and handling other chores on Branta, *the 45-foot ketch he and Jean designed and built in 1968.*

Sailing presented a real challenge. Sometimes it was scary, but I have never lost my love for it. I still sail boats myself, and I have, to my shame, three boats. I've come to like motorboats because I'm no longer agile enough to keep a sailboat going by myself.

I learned to navigate at a very early age. In fact, when I was twelve, I was often invited to go cruising by people at the yacht club, not because they wanted to have a twelve-year-old boy along but because they wanted to have a navigator for free.

While I was at school at Fieldston, which was near Columbia, Myrtle dropped me off at school as she drove to the College of Physicians and Surgeons each morning from home in New Rochelle. She'd plunk this big book in my lap and say, "Harvey, you name the muscle or the nerve, and I am going to tell you the origin and insertion and innervation that comes next to it." I learned a lot of anatomy simply by quizzing my sister.

Fieldston was distinguished for two reasons: the intellectual capability of the students, and its atrocious athletic teams. I was put on the football team to play center. About the third game I played in, I was knocked unconscious, giving me a concussion and ending my football career (probably to the benefit of the team).

However, I was the star of the ice hockey team, and we did fairly well in a league where the best was not very good. In those days one wore very little protection, and I did suffer such injuries as broken blood vessels in my lungs, but I went back to playing as soon as I was able.

[3]
Higher Education

I did terribly in high school, and I wasn't recommended to any college because I graduated in the lower fifth of my class. I've no idea why, and to this day I don't have a clue as to what happened to make me perform so badly. My teachers probably realized that I wasn't likely to make it through college, even though they had decided that I had a fairly high IQ.

What makes this more puzzling is that when I got to college, I did excellently in subjects such as mathematics and physics, subjects where you had to have a solid high school background to do well in college. I must have absorbed what I was getting in high school, because you can't go into a college course with no background and do well. So I have no idea what caused the terrible grades.

This is the story of how I got into Colgate. I applied to Colgate because my sister had been to a house party there and thought it was a pretty good place. At the time, it had recently ceased to be a Baptist theological institute. When I was interviewed by the dean of admissions, he explained to me that my faith wasn't the right one, and that he didn't think I would be admitted.

When I left, a gray-haired gentleman stopped me in the hall and said, "Are you an applicant for admission?" I said, "Yes, but I don't think I'm going to be admitted."

And he chatted with me a little while, and a few weeks later I was admitted. When I finally got to Colgate, I realized that this chance meeting in the hall was an interview by the dean of faculty. Deans of faculty are a lot more important than deans of admissions, and the dean of faculty just decided I ought to go there.

When I had finished high school, I had decided that if I was going to go to college, I'd better get more educated. So I attended Philips Exeter Academy for the summer session. Toward the end of the session, the headmaster called me in and said, "Where are you going to college?" I said, "I'm going to Colgate." He asked why, and I said, "It's the only college in the country that would admit me." He asked "Why don't you go to Harvard?" I replied that I didn't think there was the slightest chance that I'd be admitted there.

The headmaster put me in his car, took me down to Harvard, introduced me to the dean of admissions at Harvard and said, "You want to admit this man in the next freshman class."

The dean replied "Sorry, the class is full. We have a waiting list." And it turned out that I would be at the head of the waiting list.

Later, when I was told that I could be admitted to Harvard, I figured I couldn't have gone in one summer from being the dumbest kid on the block to being a Harvard student, and I subsequently decided, quite wisely, to stick to my decision to go to

Colgate. I probably could have done the work at Harvard, but Colgate was right for me at that stage.

When I was a freshman at Colgate, I developed what was diagnosed as incipient appendicitis. It was decided that I would be operated on at Presbyterian Hospital in New York City during the Christmas holiday. There ensued one of those things that don't happen in medicine these days. They did the surgery and took out my appendix. It wasn't an emergency. The chief of surgery did it just as a precautionary measure, because at Colgate you couldn't possibly get to any hospital in time, and in those days a burst appendix was a death sentence. A few days after the operation, I ran a high temperature. The doctors decided the wound was infected. A week later they performed another operation and took out about an inch, or maybe two, of my abdominal wall. The incision was held together by wires running into my abdomen and irrigated regularly with Dakin's solution, a not particularly pleasant sensation.

When I was coming out of the anesthesia, the nurse was irrigating the wound. I was in a semi-conscious state, and I knocked her across the room into the wall. Another week later, they decided to close up the wound. It had to be pulled together with very strong wire and other contraptions. I got through that all right, but about three days later, with very heavy bandaging around my midsection, the wound began to itch. That was it. I started to cry. I guess the nurse called my sister, who was in the dormitory at Columbia Presbyterian across the street, and told her to come over because they couldn't stop me from crying. My sister came over and finally got the crying to stop.

I started at Colgate really seriously worried about making the grade and ended up getting my bachelor of science degree in three-and-a-half years and graduating magna cum laude and Phi Beta Kappa. While I was there, I had expected to study to become a physician, like my sister, so I took a premedical course. The premedical curriculum required physics for a year. I signed up during my sophomore year and found the subject especially interesting.

The course was taught by a professor who was the new head of the physics department. Colgate was well-known for its wonderful football team, and among the courses that the football players took was "The History of the Pipe Organ," which they were sure to pass with an A if they played on the football team. What I didn't realize at the time was that physics was also a course they all took because the former head of the department loved football and always gave members of the team good grades.

The year I took it, the class was about five of us plus the whole football squad. It turned out that the new department head took his physics very seriously, and after the first two weeks, there were no more football players present, so it ended up being a very small class.

At the end of the year, there was an exam that I hadn't run into before or since. It was given by agreement among the physics teachers throughout the country in colleges to determine how well physics was being taught in these various institutions. Apparently I did outstandingly well, so well that I was told that I probably could get a scholarship to a very good graduate school and become a professor of physics.

This was a delightful surprise. After thinking about it, I decided, "Gee, I know I can do this. I don't know what other things I can do. Why don't I head for a career in physics?"

I announced this to my father. Several months later my father said, "Look, considering what college physics professors get paid nowadays, you're going to have an awful time providing an adequate income if you want to get married and have children. If you really want to become a professor of physics, I'll provide you with a trust fund to help supplement your income."

It took me about two weeks to conclude that I wasn't going to live on my father's money. I was going to make my own way in the world. So I decided I would continue to take physics, but I wasn't going to become a physicist.

Incidentally, low pay for physics professors isn't the norm any more. Now they get paid quite well.

The rest of that story is that now I was faced with the choice of going into medicine, in which I thought I could do well, or going into business. I knew that, although he never put any pressure on me, my father would have liked to see me go into business. My mother, on the other hand, would have liked to see me become a physics professor. I had to make the choice.

Let me make it clear that neither of my parents put any pressure on me as to what I should do. They both tried to accommodate whatever I wanted. I didn't know what business was all about, but I did know something about what medicine was about.

In college, I was a member of the Sigma Chi fraternity, which turned out to be a very good thing for me. It taught me about social life in college.

I joined the fraternity because they invited me, but unlike most of my fraternity brothers, I didn't drink much. I didn't do much partying either, and since I was taking all lab courses, I worked morning and night. So it was a great shock to me when, at the end of my junior year, I was elected president of the fraternity. However, it came in handy later in my life.

My early training at my mother's hands in memorizing and declaiming was a boon for me at Colgate, where, as a member of Mask and Triangle, I was called upon repeatedly to act in the plays the company presented. Frequently the drama coach would summon me to substitute for an actor who'd become ill or for some other reason couldn't go on. My histrionic skill may not have been impressive, but the rate at which I could learn and recite the part evidently was.

One of the more unusual insights into the way my family guided me is illustrated by the following occurrence.

I was about to return to Colgate for my junior year. At about that time, the people of the United States had accepted the fact that the prohibition against alcoholic beverages was a lost cause.

Before I left for Colgate, my father said to me, "You don't just drink alcoholic beverages. After college, there will be many occasions, either social or to do with your career, when you'll need to drink, so you must learn how to drink, and this is a good time for that. Learn how to handle liquor sensibly. Don't come home from college without knowing how to drink socially and not exceed the limit you set for yourself—or without looking like the one person in the group who doesn't drink."

Back at college, I told my fraternity brothers, whom I lived with, about my father's orders and asked for their help. Since I offered to pay for the liquor we consumed, I received a great deal of assistance. And I learned how to drink. In my life I have been drunk only once, and that was at Oxford.

I was so far out in front toward the end of my time at Colgate that when I went to register for my last semester of college and asked what I had to do to complete the requirements for graduation, they said, "Oh, you've got everything and more than is required for graduation. There's nothing you have to sign up for."

I attended Oxford more or less by accident. I didn't want to spend another six months at Colgate doing nothing, so I asked my professors for advice. One of them, who'd been at Oxford, said, "Why don't you go to Oxford? That's the university I went to." I thought that would be great. I could go to that large university and do more advanced physics during my extra time. I had already been admitted to the Harvard Business School to study for an MBA, not because I intended to become a businessman but because I at least wanted to know something about running a business.

I was admitted to St. John's College at Oxford University for autumn '36. For Harvard, I'd been admitted to the class of '38.

What was I to do?

Then I discovered that I could have my cake and eat it too. Harvard had an accelerated course that I could begin in January 1936 and finish that fall in time to get to Oxford for a full year of study there. So I left Colgate in January of '36 and completed a year at Harvard Business School in time to enter Oxford for the '36 fall semester there.

When I got to Oxford, I fully intended to carry on more physics research. Instead, I obtained a multifaceted education that proved to be invaluable but bore little resemblance to what I had expected. For example, coming from a small college in upstate New York, I was confident that a world-renowned university would offer courses in anything I could have studied at Colgate.

I didn't even bother to check the course catalogue at Oxford. I was sure that I would be able to continue the rudimentary work I had begun on X-ray crystallography, with quite a simple apparatus, at Colgate.

To my utter amazement, when I got to Oxford and asked where to find the science lab, I learned there was no such thing. This great university had almost no science facilities. It didn't have as much physics equipment as Colgate! The sciences simply weren't taught. If I'd wanted to study science I should have gone to Cambridge. Oxford taught the liberal arts, which consisted of "the greats": Greek and Latin history and literature, and ancient philosophy; and "the modern greats": philosophy, economics and politics.

In those days, you could get to Europe only by ship, and that took at least a week. Once you got there, you didn't turn right around and go home. So I decided that since I was at Oxford, I'd do what the Oxonians did: I studied the modern greats—philosophy, economics and politics.

Education at Oxford was quite different from education at an American university. Students were assigned a tutor at the college they attended. Students met with their tutor weekly but attended lectures at the various colleges daily, and used the huge, well-equipped university library—the mythical Bodleian.

It proved to be a wonderful year. I learned a tremendous amount in those subjects, which was very valuable to me later, and I developed a breadth of understanding that I wouldn't have gotten in an American college.

[4]
Rowing

At Oxford I also started rowing in an eight-oared shell. Rowing was a sport I'd never tried before, despite my love of sailing. I was asked to join the St. John's College Eight, and we had a very successful year.

Racing at Oxford is crowned by the Spring Regatta, which is a very big event indeed, with all the colleges racing against each other. Each college can enter up to three eights. The starting position of each is based on where that eight finished the year before.

Someone in authority had decided that the way to toughen up St. John's first crew would be to have them row from Oxford to London at the beginning of winter vacation. That trip, by river, is about a hundred miles, and winter in England is not a good time for wearing the standard rowing uniform of shorts and a short-sleeved shirt. Besides, it soon became painfully clear that blisters and bleeding hands, feet and bottoms were going to be rampant. So the voyage would be undertaken by the regular crew members plus a few substitutes who would sit in for those who were temporarily incapacitated by wounds or muscle cramps.

The trip started on the Isis, a tributary of the Thames that runs through Oxford. It took about three days to get to London, and we got used to having spray freeze on our legs. But the country was lovely, and we stopped every day for lunch at one of the many pubs that had a dock on the river.

Lunch came as a great relief. Attractive as the scenery was, what with Windsor and other castles and the countryside sweeping away from the river, crew members had to focus their attention on the timing of their stroke, so all we saw of our surroundings was through a series of quick peeks during the day.

Although most of the crew had to be replaced along the way, I managed to keep my wounds to a bearable level and was therefore one of the few who rowed the whole distance. It was, in retrospect, a great adventure, and an excellent preparation for Spring Regatta.

The Isis is far too narrow to race two eights abreast, as in normal races. At one time the river was narrowed even further by the ornate college barges ranked along one shore. The crew members used the barges to change from street clothes to rowing attire and back again, and the shells were stored there. Water was available on each barge, but none of it hot, except for the amount necessary to produce tea for the exhausted rowers. You had to be something of a masochist to come back to an unheated barge from a stint at rowing and then douse yourself with cold water. I was never brave—or perhaps foolish—enough to try it.

By the time I was at Oxford, the barges were gone, and each college launched its shell from a modern boathouse where all the shells were stored. Because the Isis was so narrow, a race did not begin like a traditional race, where all the shells start abreast and

Harvey, second from the right in the front row, and his St. John's crew mates at Oxford.

proceed over a fixed course. At Oxford, each shell's rudder and stern is held against the river bank. The bow is aimed diagonally upstream, carefully spaced one-and-a-half boat lengths behind the shell ahead and the same distance ahead of the shell behind it.

At the starting signal, all the shells take off from the bank, and each crew of eight attempts to catch up to the shell ahead of it and literally "bump" its bow against part of the other boat before it is bumped by the shell behind it. To score a bump, the bow of your shell has to come in physical contact with the shell ahead. Even if there is an overlap, a skillful coxswain may be able to use his rudder to prevent contact with the shell itself.

If contact is made, the bumped shell pulls to shore and drops out of the race. This means that not only does your shell have to bump the shell ahead before the end of the course, but also, if the shell ahead touches its quarry before you reach it, your only chance to score is to catch the third shell ahead of you before it catches its quarry or reaches the finish line.

This leads to a tremendous flurry of activity as soon as the race starts. It also requires that the first boat in the line-up row the full course simply to escape the boats behind it. Then it repeats the performance almost immediately as the last boat in the next-highest division.

When we bumped the boat ahead of us every day for a week, we got to be at the head of Division Two. Then we had to row the course without being bumped, and then repeat the performance the next day as the last boat in Division Two and bump the boat ahead of us. Thus we had to race twice, and win the second race an hour later.

Our team did so well that St. John's College's had a huge "bump" supper, with a great bonfire in the quad after dinner. It was an impressively inebriated celebration. Each of us on the crew received our oar, inscribed with our name and a list of the boats we had bumped. Since I rowed bow, my teammates were kind enough to give me the whole bow of an eight to take back to the United States.

Another of the things I learned at Oxford was great respect for anybody who did any job well. While at Oxford I, like everybody else, had a "scout," the man who brought me breakfast and made the bed in my very small two-room suite. He made the fire, because there was no heat in the place except the fireplace, and he also taught me how to be an English gentleman.

He did it very nicely, as a servant teaching the young man he was serving. And while he was in what might have been considered a menial position, he was an excellent and valued educator. He took a lout like me and very carefully explained, at the appropriate time, that this is what one does. He did it in a way that was neither obnoxious nor annoying, and I came to rely on my scout for advice on many things.

This was 1936. Three years later, most of the crew I rowed with at Oxford were dead. The Royal Air Force was being overwhelmed by the Germans, and each of these fellows had volunteered for the most dangerous part of the armed forces to fight for their country. Many were killed.

After my glorious year at Oxford, I returned to the Harvard Business School. My room looked out onto the Harvard Boathouse across the Charles River. After watching the rowers for a long time, I gave in to temptation. I walked across the bridge to the boathouse and asked for a boat so I too could scull. The coach asked me if I knew how to row a boat. I was somewhat indignant as I assured him that I could indeed row a boat.

The coach went over to one of the shells at the front of the dock and told me to get in and demonstrate how well I could row. I got in very gingerly while he steadied the boat by holding an outrigger. I put my feet in the stretchers and proceeded to take the boat away from the dock. I was probably a good three feet out when the boat turned over and dumped me into the muddy waters of the Charles.

Much chastened, I went inside, dried off (it was cold!) and returned. Thereupon I was assigned to one of the fixed practice craft, which were a very solid part of the dock. Practicing in the fixed shells, I graduated to something called a wherry, which was quite sturdy and broad, then to a broad comp, which looks like a shell but is more stable, and then a master comp. After many months, I finally triumphed and was allowed out in the sanctity of a real shell.

I thoroughly enjoyed sculling every time I got a chance, and I got to be pretty good, as evidenced by my winning the Harvard three-quarter-mile trophy for single sculls. Looking back at that, I realize it is the only time in my life when I had achieved something all by myself without working with one or more others. It was also the only time I entered a race because I was so charmed by the trophy, which was a very small replica of a shell.

The other sculling trophy was a complete surprise. Another student at the business school, Tom Darcy, whom I knew quite well because I "dated" his sister, suggested that we enter the double sculls race in the spring when the "Head of the Charles" race was to be held. This was a world-class race, with the best teams from the United States and Europe competing. Obviously, it was nothing that we could win, but it would be fun practicing, and an interesting experience.

The Harvard Boathouse had only two double-scull craft. Neither was a sleek, lightweight racing shell. They were both sturdy practice shells, and it was much harder to make them move fast. Since it was a race we couldn't win anyway, we were not discouraged by our equipment.

But then the impossible happened. Tom Darcy's father was an officer of the very exclusive Union Boat Club, situated just downstream from Harvard. Tom was able to convince his father that the club ought to lend us their one racing double scull so that we could practice in it and then race it. What a lovely shell it was, light, fast and sleek! After practicing in it for about a week, Tom decided that we should do a dry run of the approaching race.

The course started near Harvard and ended just beyond the Massachusetts Avenue Bridge. When racing a double scull, it is the man at the stern who sets the pace. It is the responsibility of the man forward to keep the shell on course. To do this requires looking over your shoulder at regular intervals. However, that look over the shoulder means that the person twisting has a much weaker stroke while doing so.

So when we did our practice run, it was no surprise that Tom told me that for this run I was not to turn around for the final sprint, which would start just before the bridge and carry us through to the finish line. He'd make certain that we'd stay "lined up."

We did as we had planned. All went smoothly, and we streaked right through the center of the archway of the bridge. Suddenly the boat slowed down, with a sound like tearing paper, and Tom and I, still in our seats, were sitting in the water.

When we looked around, we saw that someone had anchored a motorboat directly in the path of our beautiful shell. The shell's 8-foot-long bow had been crushed all the way to my seat.

It wasn't enough that we had wrecked the only racing shell around. It was doubtful that it could be repaired at all, and almost certainly it could not be rebuilt in time for the race. We also anticipated being lynched by the Union Boat Club members.

I don't remember how Tom managed to get us another racing shell for the race about a week later, but he worked the necessary magic. My deep concern on the day of the race was, quite seriously, that all the shells in our class would have completed the course before us and that we'd cross the finish line with some of the leaders of the next event.

To our utter amazement, we finished the race more than a full boat's-length ahead of any other shell in our class. When the judges' motorboat pulled up alongside us to invite us to the awards dinner that night, I told them that unfortunately I couldn't come because I had a date. The judges very kindly told me to bring my date along.

At the dinner we were called to accept our trophy, a huge silver cup! The top was waist-high when we stood next to it, and on it were inscribed the names of the winners of the race over the last decade. We'd actually take possession of the cup for one year after our names were added to the list.

So much for losing the race. When you are frightened that you'll end up last, it may just scare you into coming in first!

It was at Harvard that I learned to ski. This was in the days of all-wood skis and telemark turns. My first instructor was a Norwegian classmate. We drove to Mount Washington. There were no such things as ski lifts in those days, so I learned to climb with skis by trying to clamber up a narrow, steep expert trail. My instructor patiently waited until I was exhausted with the effort, and then told me he was going up to the top. His reply to my query as to how I would get down the small part of the trail that I'd just climbed was: "Just point your skis downhill. Very soon you'll fall. You'll fall on your face or your ass. If you fall on your ass, you are skiing badly. If you fall on your face, you're doing well." Then he explained how to get up so that I could repeat the performance.

After I caught my breath, I started down. The second time I got up, I sensed something going by me at express-train speed and I heard, "Good skiing, Picker. You fell on your face."

Nonetheless, his method worked, and I became a pretty good skier, good—and foolhardy—enough to do the headwall at Tuckerman's Ravine, and to ski in Switzerland, where I had a brush with an avalanche that made skiing in Switzerland thereafter much less inviting.

[5]
A Company Man

When I graduated from Harvard Business School in 1938, I decided to join Picker X-Ray. When Acme stopped selling X-ray equipment, my father had promised all his customers that he would repair the equipment and keep the machines going for as long as they had them, and my earliest job at Picker, even before I had graduated from high school, had entailed toting big, heavy pieces of obsolete Acme X-ray equipment from the third sub-basement of the building where they were stored onto an elevator and then to the street to be discarded. The sub-basement was hot and damp.

When I rejoined the company after business school, I started at the lowest level of the organization. I worked my way up through the shipping department and installation and maintenance services and then went into the office. This way I learned

Harvey started on the lowest rung at Picker X-Ray and worked his way up to the top spot, dressed accordingly.

how the business was structured and what each part of the organization did.

When I joined the company, my father told me that much as he loved me, I had to perform well at each task I was given. No preference would be shown me, and I could be fired or left where I was on the same basis as anybody else. There would be absolutely no favoritism. In fact, if anything, if I didn't become the best in the group, I was going to stay in that group. And there was no doubt in my mind that my father meant it.

That made it all the better for me. I didn't want to have a job because my father was the boss. I admired my father, and I recognized that I wasn't going to be able to do what he'd done. But I needed to know that wherever I went, I'd gotten there on my own, so I worked my way up, going through sales and all the other aspects.

I had quite a good grasp of what the company did, and what intrigued me the most was the X-ray equipment itself. Unlike my father, who had a background in pharmaceuticals, I was primarily interested in advancing the capabilities of the equipment.

I was at Colgate during Hitler's rise to power. When I read *Mein Kampf*, in German, I had become convinced that if Hitler set out to conquer Europe, he would eventually pose a real threat to the United States.

My attitude was quite unpopular on campus. It was considered un-American, especially among my fraternity brothers— even more so because we had two very handsome and affable German Nazis attending Colgate on scholarships and living in our fraternity.

The Nazis were sending students to many colleges in the United States. Along with Charles Lindbergh, who was considered a great American hero at that time, these students were very effective ambassadors for their country. They were charming gentlemen. They spoke English beautifully, and they were good-looking and very convincing.

Not surprisingly, most American students, like the American people, believed that Hitler was good for Germany. At that time, the overwhelming majority of Americans was convinced that Hitler's intentions were strictly a European affair. And having learned the lessons of World War I, they felt the United States should not become involved in any conflict that might ensue.

I was an executive of Picker X-Ray when the United States entered the war in 1941. It soon became obvious that this land war was very different from any previous land war. World War I had been fought by troops in trenches, and if the front line moved a hundred yards, that was a lot. The field hospitals that supported the troops used standard hospital equipment. It was hard to install, it was fragile, and it could take at least ten days or so to take it apart, move it and assemble it again.

On behalf of Picker X-Ray, I wrote the secretaries of the Navy and the Army to ask whether it would be desirable to try and design equipment that met the needs of this new type of warfare. The Navy wrote back, saying, "No, everything we have is fine."

The Army, on the other hand, wrote back and said that it might be interested in exploring whether more suitable equipment, such as an X-ray field unit, could be built. My response was, "If you will let us have a radiologist from the Army to advise us on how things work, and what the requirements would be for such a unit, we'll work with him to see if we can design something much more suitable for the present war." And the Army provided a colonel, who was also a radiologist.

Compare what happened then to what's done today. Picker X-Ray agreed that we would not charge the Army for any of the development work, and that we would not have exclusive rights to the design. Our one requirement was that if we produced a model that the Army liked, and if nobody underbid us, we'd get the contract to produce the machine. No military money went into the development of this completely unprecedented field unit.

Working with the people at the factory, we designed a machine that instead of being big and bulky would fit into three of the standard footlockers that were issued to every soldier. The working X-ray field unit could be assembled in less than half an hour and disassembled even faster.

It was also the first X-ray diagnostic machine that could run continuously, and that took an invention in itself. The normal X-ray tube would have given up very quickly if it didn't have time to rest. We had to develop a diagnostic tube that could run continuously so you could bring in a patient on a litter, put the litter under the X-ray tube and radiograph just as fast as you could move litters on and off.

The three footlockers that the unit was packed in could be pushed off the tailgate of a truck and not break apart. The unit came with its own power supply so it didn't have to be connected to an electrical source. It could be, as I said, reassembled and moved quickly. We subsequently developed the machine so that it could be dropped by parachute and still operate.

This allowed the machine to be close to the troops and to move as quickly as the troops did. When we developed the field unit, there was no agreement that we'd be the manufacturers. In fact, we continued to be the sole manufacturer until finally, late in the war, the military thought it was too dangerous to depend on a single manufacturer and decided to have another company make the equipment as well. That seemed logical to us, so we helped the other company learn to produce the units. They produced a few of them, but never in the massive quantities that we did.

Picker had been a small company in the manufacturing field, but this machine was supplied not only to the United States but to Russia, China, England, France—all the allies. We almost certainly produced more of these X-ray machines than all other machines that were being produced, and probably more than any other single X-ray machine that's ever been produced.

I don't think people realize the extent of the metamorphosis caused by World War II. Up to that time, as in most companies, the majority of our workers were highly skilled. As they went off to war, we had to find other people to do the work. Many women started to work in factories simply because there wasn't anybody else. And since the new workers were not highly skilled, we had to redesign the production line. The entire U.S. manufacturing industry had to modify operations in view of the fact that highly skilled workers were no longer available, but unskilled and dedicated women were.

After the war, to the utter amazement of the U.S. Government, Picker X-Ray returned $4 million to the government, representing not just part but every bit of the profits from the manufacture of the X-ray field units. It was my father's doing (at the time, I was in the Navy and at sea). While American soldiers were being killed, my father said, "We didn't want to make any profit. They were making great sacrifices. We should do our share."

It came as a complete shock to the Secretary of the Army to receive the check. Nor had the Treasury Department ever seen anything like it. Four million dollars in those days was probably equivalent to $400 million now. My father's action was considered so unusual that it was picked up by the press.

[6]

The Navy

I had felt so strongly about the United States going to war with Germany that I tried to join the Navy as an officer. It was a real struggle for me to get into the Navy reserve as a provisional ensign. The Navy saw no reason to take people who had not attended Annapolis, the naval academy. After all, the country wasn't going to get involved in the European war. Plenty of officers came out of Annapolis, and the Navy wasn't in the least bit impressed that I knew something about seamanship.

In 1940, my reserve unit was called up. The United States had not yet entered the war. We trained at Norfolk, Virginia.

One of my favorite mottos is, "If at first you succeed, quit." Among the silly jobs I was assigned while we were in training was to teach the seamen how to fire a rifle accurately. I didn't know a damn thing about the subject, but I went ahead with training our team of sailors. Somehow or other, our group tied for first place. This was very gratifying, until some stupid fellow said, "Why don't we get the trainers to break the tie?" I had never fired on that rifle range, and I thought this was a dumb idea, but I was ordered to do it. Recognizing that my reluctance was making me unpopular with the men, I went down and fired on the rifle range, and did very well—extremely well. We won, and I became somewhat of a hero to my men. But when I put the rifle down after completing the last round, I said, "I'm never going to touch a rifle on a range again! I can't repeat that. I'm not even going to try."

We were called to active duty at sea before the United States officially declared war. We were put aboard the *American Legion*, a ship that had been a transport in World War I, and ordered to take troops and supplies to Bermuda and the West Indies, where there were bases that had been leased to the United States by the British in exchange for destroyers.

The *American Legion* was located at the Brooklyn Navy Yard, and before heading out to sea, we anchored off Fort Washington, in Brooklyn Heights, to pick up ammunition to take to Bermuda. We didn't have any guns. Perhaps a better description of the *American Legion* (we called it the American Lemon) was that you could actually put your finger right through places where the rust had eaten out the deck.

One of my duties when the ship got under way was to see that the anchor was raised or lowered and securely set.

To give you some idea of the excellent condition of the ship, we had just started to raise anchor when I suddenly saw a black ball being hoisted to the masthead. This meant the ship was not under control. I called the bridge on the telephone and asked, "What's wrong?"

The answer was, "Well, we can't get up enough steam to turn the propeller, blow the whistle and raise the anchor at the same time."

Harvey as a naval person.

We went off to Charleston, South Carolina, to pick up the soldiers we were going to transport. The difference between the services in morale at that time was striking. The Navy personnel, sailors, were all volunteers or professionals. The Army soldiers had been drafted on the understanding that they'd be in for only a year and not leave the United States. They were so disaffected that they wouldn't even stand up to talk to an officer, much less salute. They were very, very sulky and angry.

On the ship, each officer's duties were decided by the captain. As a provisional ensign, I was selected as a senior deck officer, which put me in charge of the ship for four hours every day. As far as the ship's operation was concerned, during that period I was the captain's deputy on the bridge and outranked every other officer, even though I had only half a stripe and they might have as many as three or four.

My very first turn as senior deck officer occurred when we left Charleston, going to Bermuda, and I stood my first watch at sea in a hurricane. During the hurricane, the man who really knew best how to handle the ship was the navigator, who was a Norwegian. He came up to the bridge on my watch and said, "Mr. Picker, don't you think the ship is pounding very hard?" I said, "Yes, sir." But I thought, This is a hurricane, and I'd expect the ship to pound hard. He said, "Don't you think you ought to slow the ship down some?" So I respectfully replied "Yes, sir.... How do I do that?" He said, "You see those numbers up on the overhead? Those are the standard speeds. Just tell the quartermaster to crank it down." But that gives you an idea of my initial competence as a senior deck officer aboard a very large transport.

We sailed to Bermuda through the hurricane. It was awesome to see the force of the waves bend the stanchions of the rail.

We landed the first American troops on Bermuda and then proceeded down through the West Indies. At one point we couldn't steer because the steering engine failed. We were in waters infested by German submarines, and the submarines didn't care whether you were American or British or somebody else carrying things. We were completely defenseless.

In order to move the rudder and steer the ship back to Puerto Rico, we rigged two big heavy lines from the rudder post to a steam winch on either side of the ship. But on the back deck, where this operation was carried out, there was no compass and no way of knowing the rudder position. Someone on the bridge had to read the compass and the rudder position and tell you over the phone which way to move the rudder.

After a stint aft in the broiling heat, it was my turn up on the bridge. While I was there, the Norwegian navigator came up to the bridge. He looked at me as I was giving orders and he said, "Mr. Picker, I don't mind your trying to write your name in the wake, but when you go back to dot the *i*, that's going too far."

I liked sea duty, but as we sailed north, my childhood allergy to wool returned with a vengeance, and I was bleeding from various places all over my body. The ship ended up in drydock at the Brooklyn Navy Yard to be modified, and I was sent to the Brooklyn Naval Hospital to have this condition treated. The treatment only made it worse. Finally, a highly reputed dermatologist arrived. He asked, "You had this when you were a child?"

"Yes," I replied.

Then he asked, "Do you know how to deal with this?"

"Yes." I replied.

He told me to go home, take care of it and come back in ten days.

I went home, dealt with it and came back a week or so after Pearl Harbor, when I was told that I was being invalided out of the Navy as unfit for duty. "This is a mistake," I told my superior officers. "You have a real shortage of officers with knowledge of sea duty. I can stay in the Navy and replace somebody from the naval academy who is now doing a task ashore."

They gave me a pass to Washington, D.C., and a week to find a job. I had several interviews, but I didn't find anything that I considered reasonably constructive.

For example, one department wanted me to take on the duty of purchasing X-ray equipment. My response was that I could be of more use producing the equipment than purchasing it.

[7]
The Rad Lab

Every time I got through an interview, I had to report back to a receptionist. One day the receptionist suggested that I go to the Bureau of Ordnance. I replied, "The only thing I know about ordnance is which end of the gun you don't want to be in front of when it goes off." Finally, on the last day, in desperation, I went up to the Bureau of Ordnance and spoke to the officer there. After a bit, he asked me to wait a minute, and then he took me in to see an admiral. I was very impressed by this gruff and not very large man with a lot of gold braid on his uniform.

The admiral, who was in charge of the First Naval District, chatted with me for a while and then asked "How would you like to work on a super-secret project?" This was like asking a kid if he'd like a piece of candy.

Even the name of the project is confidential, the admiral told me. "If you reveal it in public, you will go to prison." Then he proceeded to explain to me that a new device, called radar, was being developed at the radiation laboratory at MIT. How would I like to work on that? Obviously I bit, hook, line and sinker!

I had the physics and some of the electronics background for the job, and it looked like a good fit. I went off to a school in Boston, Massachusetts, run by MIT, to learn the basics. Two days before school ended, I was ordered to go see the admiral again. We talked for a while and then he said, "How would you like to do research at MIT?"

This was heaven. If I couldn't be at sea, I wanted that kind of work. I said I would love to do it but that I already had orders to go back to the Bureau of Ships. So, much as I preferred to work at MIT, I had to go to Washington. The admiral said, "Come back here tomorrow." The next day he handed me orders to report to the Radiation Lab at MIT.

The Rad Lab, as it was known, was where modern microwave radar was developed and initially produced. As Robert Buderi says in *The Invention that Changed the World: How a Small Group of Radar Pioneers Won the Second World War and Launched a Technological Revolution*, "The atomic bomb only ended the war. Radar won it."

For me, these four years were a dream assignment. I was working with the very top physicists in the world, people like Enrico Fermi and Hans Bethe. I got a tremendous education in the latest circuitry and excellent insight into other developments. For example, we developed almost every use of radar that there is—though I have to admit that we never thought of microwave ovens.

We developed a radar that allowed Allied bombers flying to Germany to see the terrain so they could tell where they were going. But a radar image is very different from a visual image, and our challenge was to make it possible for the pilot or the radar operator to use radar to determine where he was. The problem was solved when somebody finally realized that since ultrasound waves move so slowly compared to the radiation from a radar set, an ultrasound crystal attached to a radar in a large tank of water, with a miniature relief of German terrain and cities at the bottom, could function as a radar scanner. It would show you what you would see flying over Germany, yet the model readily fit into a water tank about the size of a billiard table.

Another project I worked on at the Rad Lab demonstrates how greatly I benefited by understanding the possibilities of ultrasound. As the American fleet prepared to invade Japan, the Japanese resorted more and more to kamikaze planes. The pilots of these suicide planes flew low over the water, and because radar waves travel in a straight line, the curvature of the earth prevented them from being detected until it was too late. By the time the ship knew the planes were coming, men couldn't get to their battle stations to fire on them. We had to find a way to see the planes coming from a lot farther off. How could that be done?

It could be done by setting up a big radar antenna high enough so the planes could be detected in time to have the ship's antiaircraft guns manned and pointed in the right direction. Obviously the crew couldn't remain at battle stations all day and night—they had to get some rest—so what was required was an early warning system for the ships. As the Navy's man at the Rad Lab, I interpreted the Navy's needs and capabilities for the scientists so that whatever device they worked on would actually fit into an existing ship or plane.

I and a very good friend, a very bright young physicist, worked on the project. My liaison status required me to go to Washington, D.C., fairly regularly to explain new developments at the lab that might lead to improved or different devices, including how they might be applied.

The early warning system was probably the largest and most important project in which I became heavily involved. The experimental model, which was really a series of multiple systems, was built on top of Mount Cadillac, in Maine. The radar antenna had to be very high to be able to see over the horizon. That meant putting it into an airplane. But the antenna also had to be very large so it could focus the beam on a single fighter plane at a long distance and still be able to detect the very small attenuated reflection of the plane. It was a breakthrough when we discovered that an airplane could be designed and built that would fly safely even if the antenna was housed in a dome that was much wider than the plane's fuselage. Therefore we could now place our large antenna as high as a plane could fly.

The way the system was designed, the antenna and other controls of the radar had to be aboard the ship, not in the airplane. So there had to be a remote up-link and down-link.

Many of the naval officers I briefed on the project in Washington doubted that the system would be reliable enough to use, because it needed to enable aircraft controllers to see everything that could be seen on the radar, and the ship's combat control crew had to be able to determine where the radar was aimed and on what it would focus.

We needed five hundred radio tubes to accomplish this. As everyone in the Navy knew, radio tubes were reliable about 95 percent of time. This meant that we could expect about 25 tubes not to be working at any one time.

We decided the only way to convince the Navy that our early warning system was the solution to the kamikaze problem was to use this handmade experimental set to demonstrate to high-ranking Navy and Army officers concerned with this project, or with the defense of ships, how the system worked. We hoped the experimental model we built would work for the demonstration.

I was assigned to talk the Army into sending small planes toward Mount Cadillac from over the horizon, and to convince the Navy to send in destroyers from over the horizon. Obviously, with the war needing all the forces we had, this wasn't easily done.

The Navy, with a notable lack of enthusiasm, sent a number of experts and high-ranking officers to observe the demonstration. Our experimental device had its quirks, and we hoped it would work. It worked so well, in fact, that Navy personnel decided they were badly in need of it, and they wanted about 20 sets "today."

It was quite clear, however, that it would take months to convert our handmade model to a design suitable for normal production by a commercial company.

To hasten production, the Navy wanted these devices to be built in the Radiation Lab so that we could safeguard the ships in the Pacific as quickly as possible. Dr. Walt Dyke, a good scientist and a very close and dear friend of mine, and I were assigned to develop the process of producing acceptable units until a commercial supplier could take over supplying the units to the Navy.

This put terrible pressure on us. Every time we'd read about a cruiser being sunk by a kamikaze and hundreds of men killed, we felt that it was our fault, that if we'd gotten the needed units out there, those men wouldn't have died. The pressure was so great that Walt suffered a nervous breakdown that made him incapable of functioning.

I succeeded in getting through this period, and in 1945 the first few sets of what became known as AWACS (Airborne Warning and Control System) were built and functioned quite effectively.

Much earlier in the war, England was almost incapacitated by the effectiveness of German submarine warfare against transatlantic shipping. The introduction of microwave radar, developed at the Rad Lab, decimated the German submarine force so effectively that I was later told by a German naval officer that being assigned to a submarine was regarded as the equivalent of being condemned to die within two weeks.

This was because German submarines were no longer safe even if all they showed above the surface of the water was a periscope. Microwave radar made it possible to see and attack them as they came up for air or when they were running below at periscope depth.

Many other devices were developed early on, such as having radar aim the antiaircraft guns on ships. The radar would pick up an incoming plane, even in clouds, so that the ship's guns were aimed automatically. Later, these gun mounts could be directed with even more accuracy because the system was improved to compensate for the pitch and roll of the ship.

Radar was not only a remarkably effective weapon against the enemy, it also saved many Allied lives. I remember an evening when, over cocktails, someone wondered, "If radar can tell us, even in bad weather, where a plane is to shoot it down, why can't we use it to help a wounded pilot or a damaged plane to land?" An effective system for helping desperately damaged planes or pilots land much more safely, as well as reducing the danger of ship collisions at sea, was developed.

[8]
Developing Picker X-Ray

After the war ended, my experience was invaluable at Picker X-Ray. The X-ray field unit Picker had designed and manufactured proved so reliable that radiologists returning from the war sought out Picker equipment. This was to have huge consequences for the company, of which I had become chief executive in 1945.

Some years after the war, thinking about how radar might apply to medical diagnosis, I realized, as did others, that the human body is mostly water, and that maybe you could use ultrasound to see what went on inside the body.

Some of my acquaintances from the Rad Lab put a human being inside a big tank filled with water and moved the radar-type transmitter/receiver around in the tank to see what could be seen inside the person.

It proved that it could show you the internal parts of the person, though the image was extremely coarse. As time went by, the device improved to where it could show a fetus in a woman.

In those days, X-ray was the only way to see whether the fetus's head could pass through the mother's pelvis. By that time, we knew that it wasn't particularly good for the infant, or the mother, to be examined by X-ray, but that was the only way to do it.

It occurred to me that diagnostic ultrasound would be a great product for our X-ray company to sell to radiologists. Radiologists already knew how to read images, and they would recognize the fact that everyone was better off not using X-rays.

Working with the group that had done the early experiments, we were the first organization to go into the business of making ultrasound equipment.

The X-ray field fascinated me because it represented the interaction between medicine and developments in electrical engineering, mechanical engineering and physics. The big trick, I learned later, was to combine the different fields and look for ways to innovate, giving you the necessary ingredients to get ahead of the curve. No one person did all these things. We had a remarkable group of development engineers at Picker X-Ray, quite open to trying new, and sometimes seemingly foolish, ideas. In fact, we held a development meeting every month or two to discuss what needed to be improved or what new developments should be pursued.

At the end of a long day of discussions, we'd adjourn the meeting, have cocktails or beer and then hold a brainstorming session. The rule was that no idea was too silly to consider. Some very innovative ideas from these sessions were successful. On the other hand, a lot more were not even pursued.

Let me say a little here about finances. I ran Picker, unlike many modern organizations, on principles that I learned from my father. One of these was that in order to survive, you had to make a minimum profit every year, and you had to know what this was. But you also had a maximum profit. If you made more than that, you were either underpaying your employees or not putting enough money into research. So I didn't focus on quarterly results. My objective was to plan for five years of healthy growth.

Picker X-Ray was the first company to build radioactive therapy machines by using fission, or the radiation from cobalt 60. I was familiar with cobalt 60 because we at the Rad Lab knew about the very secret "pile" in Chicago where some new radioactive elements were being developed. I had wanted Picker to build that kind of machine because it would provide more effective radiation therapy more reliably and less expensively. Each time we had a development committee meeting, I had suggested that we assign some engineers to develop this idea, but my recommendations went nowhere.

As a result, in the early 1960s I hired a whole new section of engineers to develop cobalt-60 and other radioactive therapy machines to treat tumors in human beings. And then, having invested a great deal of money to design these devices, and more money to produce a factory to manufacture them—as well as a "hot" lab to receive, store and load the cobalt into the machines—I discovered that GE had built one for a hospital in Texas.

I wasn't surprised to discover that GE had received a government contract to build one machine, but I was stunned by a subsequent announcement that GE would not build any more. I had bet the ranch with a huge investment to build these devices. Although I believed that they were much safer, simpler and better for use in treating humans than the normal high-voltage X-ray therapies, now it appeared that GE knew something I didn't.

Clearly, we were headed for a disaster. But there was nothing I could do to alter course. We were so far into the project that we felt we might as well go on and finish it. We finished it.

It turned out to be very successful, and nobody else in the United States was building these devices. Our only competition was a company supported by the Canadian government.

Another of the things I wanted the company to look into was anesthesia. Up until then, anesthesia was extremely dangerous for patients because the anesthetic used could damage the lungs. Someone who was anesthetized with ether for too long could became quite ill and die. Alternatively, something like cyclopropane could be used, instead of ether, but it presented its own great danger. Cyclopropane was much safer for the patient and far less damaging to the lungs. But it was very explosive. And if there was a spark in the room, cyclopropane made a bomb out of the patient. The patient could literally explode and kill the other people in the room too.

We took on the project of building an X-ray machine that was "explosion-proof." We finally devised a way to produce a machine that could be used safely in an explosive atmosphere, and we sent it over to be tested by the board of underwriters. The board got the machine and said, "Now, how do we test it? We don't have any protocol for it, so we don't know how to test it." We suggested a protocol that was accepted. We had produced the first X-ray machine you could use safely with cyclopropane.

Another idea related to anesthesia that I explored was the Polaroid Land camera. Because anesthesia was very dangerous to the patient when used for any length of time, the operation to set a fractured hip for an older person had a high mortality rate just from the devastating effect of anesthesia.

Prolonged anesthesia could be very dangerous. When I was a boy, I had to have an operation for an inguinal hernia. Searching for someone to perform this rather simple operation, my father decided on a surgeon who could do the whole operation in eight minutes. The fact that he could do the operation in much less time than anyone else pre-empted all other considerations. There was anesthesia—it was ether—but there was very little because the operation went so quickly.

Hip operations were very slow because, first, a radiograph had to be taken to show the position of the broken parts of the head of the femur. It then took at least 10 minutes of waiting time for the film to be developed so it could be read. Then, when the surgeon believed he had approximated the position of the broken ends, another radiograph was needed, requiring another interlude of about 10 to 15 minutes. If the two parts of the bone were in the right position, a guide was inserted into the head of the femur. That too required being checked by a radiograph. And the process was repeated after the nail had been inserted to assure it was aligned correctly to be driven into the remainder of the femur. Finally, if all was properly aligned, the nail was driven and a final radiograph was needed to be certain that everything was in order. The time under anesthesia waiting for X-rays to be developed was several hours, adding greatly to the danger. How could all that waiting time for X-ray films to be developed be greatly shortened?

My objective was to produce a device that could be used for hip operations for elderly people, since most broken hips were sustained by older people, who were also the most vulnerable to the anesthesia. The idea struck me that perhaps the popular Polaroid camera and film might be the answer. I knew Ed Land, the inventor and the head of Polaroid. I went to him and said, "Ed, will Polaroid work for X-rays?"

"I don't know, but I think it would," he answered.

Then I asked, "Could you build a camera that's big enough to be able to show a whole hip on it?"

He replied, "We've never tried it."

Ed and I agreed on a working relationship. He would try to produce a Polaroid film that was big enough to take a picture of a hip, and Picker X-Ray would undertake to create a process to spread the gel evenly over the whole film so it would develop properly.

Our partnership was successful, and after an awful lot of mistakes we got it right. All this was produced to improve hip surgery.

This was during the Cold War, when the people and the government were greatly concerned about the danger of a nuclear war breaking out between the United States and the Soviet Union.

If that were to happen, the United States would face the problem of how to provide emergency medical care to the affected population. Conventional X-ray film would have been ruined by any nuclear explosion because the radiation would spread over a very large area.

However, this would not be true of the Polaroid-Picker device and film, which didn't need liquid processors. The system would still be operable as well as faster to use. The film could be stored indefinitely in caves or in cellars and would not be sensitive to radiation until it was sensitized for use.

The military got wind of these devices and films and put away large stores for use in case of a nuclear attack, which we all thought might happen. That's one more discovery that grew out of all my great contacts.

During the Korean War, when we improved the mobile X-ray field unit even more, we gave the profits back to the government, just as my father had done in World War II. My decision was based on an ethic that was very important first to my father and then to me: We were not going to make a profit while Americans were giving their lives for the United States.

I got tremendous satisfaction from the work we did. Everything we produced reduced human suffering, added to life expectancy or produced scientific knowledge of use in research. We didn't produce anything other than what was beneficial to humans.

Back in the early days of television—it must have been the middle or late 1950s—it was discovered that a GE television set produced X-rays that irradiated little children sitting on the floor in front of the television set. This caused a huge furor. It happened not because of any failing by the X-ray industry; the fault lay with the television industry.

Congress set out to write radiation protection laws. This, of course, would have a great effect on machines that produced X-rays.

When hearings on the legislation were held, I said I wanted to go to Washington to testify. Picker X-Ray's lawyers said, "You mustn't do that, because you can't use an attorney to defend yourself in these hearings. They're going to go at you, and you'll end up in a terrible amount of trouble."

I said, "Yes, I understand that. On the other hand, I know a great deal about radiation and its effects, as well as what is being done to protect the doctors, nurses and patients who are the group most affected by this problem. I've been heavily involved in radiation protection for them. Congress needs somebody who really knows what he's talking about."

So I volunteered, and the Senate committee invited me down to testify. I gave them accurate statistics on the rate at which the X-ray industry itself, without any urging from any outside source, had reduced dangerous and unwanted stray radiation, and I listed the ways in which we had progressed. I told the committee how much better today's machine was than it had been five or ten years earlier, and I said, "If you're going to legislate on this, one of the things you mustn't do is legislate by saying it must be done this way. That will stop all progress, and the technology will be up-to-date now but not in the future. If you do legislate, you need to take into account that we're learning more and more about how to provide better protection."

One of the senators said to me, "Machines are so much better now than machines produced seven or eight years ago. Shouldn't we require that all hospitals have new equipment?"

"That would be wonderful for Picker X-Ray, and I'd love it," I replied. "It would give us a bigger boost than anything I could think of. But doing that will be a big expense to the hospitals and to the healthcare industry. Just legislate the standards so that machines over seven years old, for example, have to be brought up to standard. But don't clamp down on it and cause a huge rise in the cost of healthcare, because it isn't going to be that important."

The Senate committee and I got along beautifully. They appeared to find my comments very interesting, and I enjoyed testifying. It was one more example of being able to use my knowledge for making things turn out well.

Of course, you tend to remember your successes and not your failures, and I made huge mistakes, too. As chief executive, I had a better chance to make big mistakes than anybody else in the company, and I took full advantage of my opportunities to do so.

As computers began to be widely used, I made the mistake of deciding that the company should manufacture small computers. We had a staff that knew how to make the computers that were needed for some of the nuclear instruments we were manufacturing, so I decided that we would produce not only those computers but also ones for independent use. We started out doing fairly well, making and selling them.

Then catastrophe struck. A large number of the computers we made failed very soon after being put to use. The failure proved to be that of a key component supplied to us by GE. That meant we had to buy back every one of those computers.

There were other failures. There had been a great deal of effort to improve high-voltage radiation-therapy machines. They were very big and very bulky, and they had to be motor-driven to be positioned properly. We developed a very light and flexible machine that could be focused easily by hand. This meant that the oncologic radiologist could position the machine faster and more accurately. It also benefited patients because the machine could be aimed more quickly and accurately.

These machines worked quite satisfactorily, but they required a very unusual tube to generate the X-rays. The manufacturer, Westinghouse, produced a small quantity of these special tubes, and they worked very well. But then Westinghouse somehow lost the technique and was never again able to make tubes that worked, despite much effort on their and our part. They finally shut down production and we lost the whole development.

[9]

Jean

My first meeting with Jean Sovatkin, in 1946, should have prevented us from ever seeing each other again. My mother had met one of Jean's aunts at a summer resort. The aunt said she had a niece whom I should meet, so a meeting was arranged for sometime during the winter. I was about thirty-one. The evening I was supposed to meet Jean for the first time, my parents came from Florida on the train, which was the major means of transportation in those days. I went to Pennsylvania Station to pick them up. Then we went to the Hotel Pierre, where Jean's aunt and uncle were staying and where I was going to meet Jean. When we got to the Pierre, my mother decided, "We'll go up with you and see Jean's aunt and uncle."

So I arrived for my first date with Jean with my parents in tow. I'm sure Jean couldn't help wondering what kind of guy

Jean and Harvey doing some of their favorite things, including dancing (every week at the Waldorf Astoria's Starlight Roof).

comes to meet her for the first time and brings his mother and father along. The adults appeared to enjoy themselves, but Jean and I had little to say. Then the older folks went off and left Jean and me to ourselves. We started to chat, and I must have been remarkably obnoxious, because I remember Jean saying to me, "Harvey, why don't you take that pipe out of your mouth and stop pontificating?"

I took Jean out to dinner and brought her back, thinking, She is a fairly nice person. I tried three times to arrange another date with her, but each time she couldn't make it. I took that to mean that she was never going to make it. So I proceeded to forget that one; I knew other women who weren't so busy.

I was very surprised when Jean called and invited me to dinner. She told me to meet her at the 21 Club. When she came out to the reception desk, she told me the name of some man she'd just had drinks with. I wasn't au courant enough with the motion picture business to realize that she'd just had cocktails with some very important actor. When she talked about someone named Gary (in fact, it was Gary Cooper), it took a while—years, in fact—for me to figure out what was happening and where she was working.

Jean had a fascinating background. She was born in Brooklyn and attended Smith College. After she graduated, she went to work for *Life* magazine as a researcher. She eventually became a correspondent and a member of the editorial board.

Life subsequently sent her to Las Vegas, the only place that had gambling in the country, to learn about and report on gambling. She worked for one of the gambling houses as a shill, the person who sits at the table and appears to be gambling so the table won't be empty, but uses money that belongs to the house. As a result, she became a very good gambler. And since she was working with the outstanding photographers of that time, she learned to be a very good photographer.

Another of the assignments *Life* gave Jean was to follow an Air Force bomber training group from the time they were inducted into the Army to the time they left for Europe to fight. (Only one person out of that crew survived.) They had a great time, and everyone was tickled by the idea of a woman in training camp. They had to take a physical, and Jean told the story of being in line with the men, all of them stripped naked, and she wearing a towel. She worried about what would happen when she got to the doctor, but fortunately the doctor was sensitive enough to say, Just go on and I'll see you later.

After going dancing and skiing and doing things like that together, Jean and I were pretty well ready to think seriously about getting married. When *Life* got the rights to publish Winston Churchill's books about World War II, Jean was asked to go to England and interview Churchill and, on the same trip, the great actor Laurence Olivier.

Jean was very friendly with Carlotta Oppenheimer, whose husband, Bobby, was the head of the DeBeers diamond syndicate. Carlotta was in the United States on a visit, and we all had dinner together frequently. One evening Carlotta said to me, "Look, I know you and Jean are thinking about getting married, but don't let that interfere with Jean's coming over to England to interview Churchill, because if you do she will always regret having passed up a superb opportunity." It sounded sensible to me; certainly it was more important to talk to Churchill than to me.

A few nights before Jean was due to sail to Europe—there were no flights; you didn't fly back and forth in those days—it got to be too much for me, and I asked her to marry me. She said, "You should have thought about that sooner. I'm going to England, and if you really want to do something, I'll consider it."

She went off to England. After about two-and-a-half months, as she was getting toward the end of her assignment, I began spending the huge amount of money required to call her frequently. When I asked her to come home and talk about getting married, her reply was typical. "Talk about it, no. I'm not coming. Either we are getting married or we're not."

I recognized her superior reasoning and said "Let's get married."

Jean was staying at Carlotta and Bobby's house in London. She told Carlotta that she was going home to get married. The next morning Bobby came down and gave her what looked like an unusually large sugar cube wrapped in a piece of tissue paper. "This is a wedding present from Carlotta and me," he said.

Jean looked at the large object and asked what it was.

"That's an uncut diamond," Bobby replied.

Jean handed it back to him, saying, "Oh, thank you, but I couldn't. Harvey wants to give me my engagement ring." The price of good manners. Jean ended up with a diamond which was about a tenth the size of what it could have been.

Jean and I were married in 1947. We had two children and, as we planned, had them fairly close to each other. Our daughter Frances, known as Bobbi, and our daughter Gale are both very happily alive, married to fine men and doing good things. Bobbi is married to Tim Hamill. Together they run what may be one of the largest collections and gallery of West African art and artifacts in this country. And Gale is married to John Larsen, a senior pilot for the big Alaskan cruise ships, a very competent man. They live in Seattle with their two daughters.

In 1953, Jean started working as a volunteer in the United Nation's Office of Public Information. Her job was primarily to brief American visitors in the gallery just before sessions started, telling them the background of what had gone on in this or that particular committee, the matters that were being considered and who the participants were and what their general attitudes were. This required being familiar with all the aspects of these meetings.

Some Picker family activities.

In 1958 Jean became a member of the UN Committee of Correspondence, which trained women from poorer countries for leadership roles.

Earlier, Jean had done a lot of work for Westchester County. We lived in Larchmont, New York. This was at a time where people were really worried about a nuclear exchange between the Soviet Union and the United States. Jean worked on a committee that made plans for evacuating New York City. She wrote a booklet about Westchester County and how it operated. It was so good that the county bought the rights and distributed a copy to everyone who lived there. Depending on different editions, the booklet was between ten and twenty-five pages long. When Jean was working at the UN, she got the idea of doing the same thing about the UN.

We had gotten to know Eleanor Roosevelt. My mother had met her through their work in women's suffrage. Mrs. Roosevelt had lunch at my mother's house. (Jean was invited; I wasn't.) In 1955, when Mrs. Roosevelt was serving as the United States delegate to the UN Social and Economic Committee, Jean suggested that she and Eleanor write a book, *The United Nations: What You Should Know About It*. This was the first collaboration between the two. It was a very, very successful book and eventually translated into 15 languages. Both Jean and Eleanor believed deeply in the mission of the UN, and they remained close friends until Eleanor's death in 1962.

Here is another example of a simple occurrence that was to have vast repercussions. In 1968, Jean got a call: "Mrs. Picker, Lyndon Johnson, the President of the United States, has to appoint somebody as a delegate to the UN Social and Economic Committee, and your name has been suggested. I'd like to ask you to consider whether you would be willing to undertake this task, and since the President feels that it is fairly urgent to make this appointment, I hate to rush you but I'd like your decision within the next ten days. Would you please call me back?"

And, typical of Jean, she said, "I don't have to call back. I'll take it." In later years, we've discovered how the President had decided to invite her. It turned out that the President had asked six different people to suggest a replacement for Mrs. Roosevelt's job, and everyone on the list selected Jean. The UN was to be a major part of Jean's life.

[10]
Aloft

I'd performed multiple tasks during World War II. One of them was testing aircraft radar. There was a fighter plane called the Black Widow. The entry to the compartment for the radar operator was through a trapdoor on the floor. The radar operator sat on one side and shifted for landing to the other side of the trapdoor. I was checking out the radar when we came in for a landing. We were probably not more than a hundred feet above the runway, and I moved from one seat to the other to strap myself in. In doing so I stepped on the trapdoor. It opened. Fortunately, I was able to grab the arm of the chair and climb back up. The sensation of hanging by your hands, and other events like that, made me think I hated airplanes.

I'd had to do a lot of flying in running Picker, and I complained bitterly to Jean, who had gotten her pilot's license in college. Jean suggested that I learn to fly, an experiment that I tried, and I ended up totally cured when I discovered how completely safe flying really is.

One day my flight instructor and I were in a light, single-engine plane. Suddenly he reached over and turned off the ignition, shut the engine down, took the key out and said, "Now what are you going to do?"

That scared the hell out of me. But I found that I was still flying. I could still control the plane, and we weren't going to have to land for quite a while. The plane was going to go down slowly, but it wasn't going to drop like a stone, and there was plenty of time to look around and decide where to land. The instructor said, "See if you can land on that golf course without killing some golfers."

After that and many other things, I discovered that I no longer had a problem with flying. These small planes were very good, very stable and very safe, and I ended up getting myself a little single-engine plane. Then I got a twin-engine plane and my instrument rating so I could fly a multi-engine plane in any kind of weather. I did fly a great deal, and I enjoyed it. The only trouble with flying a plane is you are inside the plane, away from the sunshine.

[11]

Picker and CIT

In 1958, Jean and I faced a problem. Almost all my assets were in Picker X-Ray stock. My wife was a brilliant and wonderful woman, but her own career had not included much experience in running a company.

If I made the mistake of dying, the taxes would be very high, and Jean wouldn't have any liquid assets with which to pay them except Picker stock, which was privately held. That meant she would have to try to sell the stock of a closely held company that had just lost its CEO.

I set out to see what we could do about separating my income and assets from the fate of Picker X-Ray. One way would have been to list the company on the New York Stock Exchange. But I didn't want to face the prospect of trying to explain to stockholders why I was spending money on foolish projects that could turn out to be disasters. As I've said, I wasn't a damn bit interested in how we did quarterly. I was interested in where we would be in five years, and the stock exchange tendency to focus on how much we made in the last quarter and how much we were going to make in the next was far from anything I could be interested in.

The next best thing was to find a large organization with publicly owned stock that would take over the company. We talked to some of the leading companies in the electronics field, several of them very good, and found they were all interested in acquiring Picker X-Ray. It also became obvious that they all had very strong ideas about how it should be run. I didn't want that—I wanted to continue to run the thing. I was having a hell of a good time doing it.

So I wanted to find a company that would own Picker stock and let me run the operation. Quite by chance, my mother had fallen into conversation with a woman at a resort where she was staying. It turned out that my mother was talking to the wife of the head of CIT Financial, a very large and very successful conglomerate of companies that produced an array of products ranging from greeting cards to earth-moving equipment.

CIT was interested. CIT had a very stable stock and steady sales, but no one there knew a damn thing about the X-ray business. Nor did they want to know anything about it (I have to say that I had the same attitude toward CIT's various bank holdings and other businesses), but they were interested in acquiring the stock. It seemed to be a very happy solution. I would remain as CEO of Picker X-Ray, CIT would exchange Picker stock for CIT stock and Jean would have something she could sell to pay the taxes if I died.

CIT was interested only in whether Picker made money, so I could explain to CIT, not the stockholders, why I made those damn-fool mistakes. With the help of my great friend Sam Butler and, later, Christine Beshar and her other colleagues at Cravath,

Swaine & Moore in New York, I sold Picker to CIT in 1958. I ran Picker X-Ray until 1965. CIT seemed quite pleased with the results, and I served on the CIT board from 1968 to 1981. In 1967 the company's name was changed to Picker Corporation.

People have asked me what it was like to work for someone else. Before, I couldn't be fired; now I could. My reply was—and this is something I truly believe—that if while I was running Picker X-Ray I found someone who could do a better job, I would immediately put him or her at the top and get out. It was no different with CIT. If CIT could find someone better than me to run the company, they should do it. Once you have a company running, you want it to be run as well as possible.

About three or four years after the sale, CIT very wisely looked for someone to be my successor in case something happened to me. This was fine with me. In fact, I'd about decided that I'd run Picker long enough. I was getting stale and didn't have as many innovative ideas as I once did. I had worked hard over the previous three or four years to develop successors for myself. I did develop two, both of them good, and in 1965, with CIT's blessing, I resigned as the chief executive officer.

[12]

The Hudson Institute

I was, however, engaged in a lot of other activities, including working in a number of nonprofit organizations. One of them was the Hudson Institute.

Around 1950, soon after the nuclear bomb had been developed and tested, a friend of mine suggested that I chat with a visitor from California, Herman Kahn, a military strategist and systems theorist who worked at the Rand Corporation, a major American think tank. Herman's ideas about the place of nuclear weapons in the world were very like my own, though further advanced.

Jean and I discussed what this very bright man was working on. We decided to fund him in something that became the Hudson Institute, and I wasn't surprised when he invited me to be a member of his board.

These events led to the first real analysis of the place of a nuclear weapon in warfare. It was clear that Herman didn't look at it the same way as the U.S. and Soviet armies. They regarded it simply as a bigger bomb.

Herman, on the other hand, realized that it was a device whose role needed to be radically rethought. On analysis, it wasn't just a bigger bomb. It had to be redefined in terms of how it could be used both in diplomacy and as a weapon. We spent a lot of time deciding that this was a weapon that could be used not in regular warfare but as something that could influence political outcomes. That's too short an account, but it was the gist of our thinking.

Herman and I explained this new view to the U.S. government and the U.S. military, and they finally understood and agreed with us. We then said, "Now we're going to tell the Soviet Union the same thing." The U.S. military said, "No, no. This is secret. You shouldn't discuss it with them."

Our argument was different. It was that if you're following a course of action, the Soviets need to know what it is so they could include it in their thinking about how to look at nuclear weapons.

It wasn't terribly difficult to discuss this with the Soviets. As a result, Herman was invited to Moscow for high-level talks. While these did not immediately lead to an agreement between the United States and the Soviet Union, they became the basis of the attitudes that led to the Nuclear Non-Proliferation Treaty being enacted in 1968.

This was during the Cold War, when both countries were snarling at each other, and the Soviets saw the sense of looking at things the way Herman did, which is what really led to the agreements about nuclear weapons that have been promulgated since then. If you were to "use" a nuclear weapon "thoughtfully," it would only be as a trade-off of one bomb by each side. Hudson

Institute actually was a major force in generating current attitudes about nuclear weapons, their proliferation and their use. It was one of the first entities to realize that nuclear power had made the world very different from what it had been.

[13]

A Student Again

In 1965, I was 50 years old, and I'd decided that I'd been doing what I was doing long enough. It occurred to me that I could go back to the other big thing in my life that I had contemplated—teaching physics. But physics is a young person's game, and you don't get into it when you're 50 years old.

I started wondering what life would have been like if I'd become a professor. One of my friends on the board of directors of the Hudson Institute, Bill Fox, was a professor at Columbia University in the Graduate School of International Affairs, and I asked him if he thought I could get accepted as a candidate for a Ph.D., even though I was a superannuated student. And Bill said, "Well, yes, if you want to, come try it." So I was admitted to Columbia as a doctoral candidate.

I made this decision after serious contemplation. I wanted a different kind of challenge and a completely different career. I was very interested in my work with the Hudson Institute, and in the work Jean was doing at the UN.

In 1967, President Johnson appointed me to the U.S. National Science Board. This organization not only runs the National Science Foundation but sets science policy for the U.S. government. There was a lot of activity during all this period, and it was exciting to be working with so many interesting people. The foundation built a base in Antarctica and provided the funds and direction to build the first deep-sea drilling rigs, which led to the discovery of large oil fields in the Caribbean. I thoroughly enjoyed the appointment.

Then fate played a nasty trick on me. Within a year of my resignation from CIT, my first successor dropped dead of a heart attack. But we still had another string to our bow, and the other candidate was installed. About a year after he was installed, he developed terminal cancer. I guess I could have said that was no longer my problem, but I went back to the job of running Picker until we could find a successor.

In 1968, I was doing three jobs. I was on the National Science Board, which required real work. I was a full-time student at Columbia, and I was trying to run Picker X-Ray. One evening, Jean got a phone call, saying, "Your husband is lying on the floor of the men's room at Columbia and can't get up. What do you want us to do about it?" You know, it's quite something for your wife to be presented with a situation like this when she's in the town of Larchmont and you're thirty-five miles away in the men's room at Columbia.

Jean said, "I'll get an ambulance." They wanted to take me to the hospital and I said, No, I'm going home. I insisted, so they, with misgivings, took me home. It turned out that the stress of trying to do three jobs was probably more than I could handle, and I had experienced a very severe panic attack.

The doctor who took care of me at home said, "Well, there's nothing we can do for this, but it will go away." Panic attacks disabled me almost completely for about six months or more. I was terrified if Jean left the room. Finally, by resting and not working, I recovered. But it was at least three years before I could function fully again.

I started working again part-time at the end of the six months. I finished up my term on the National Science Board and then focused primarily on being a student.

I also served on the Colgate board of trustees. As a matter of fact, when I later became a faculty member, I resigned from the board because Colgate had no precedent of having a faculty member on the board. Although I think they would have readily kept me as a trustee, I didn't want to set that precedent, and I wanted to be a faculty member more than I wanted to be a trustee.

One thing that stands out now from that experience so many years ago was that blacks began to be admitted to white colleges. When I was on the board, Colgate went through the procedure that almost every other college did. At first, blacks were a kind of token. They were looked upon as desirable if admitted in small numbers. As more and more blacks were admitted and became a larger proportion of the classes, they did what they did in almost every other organization. They coalesced. They wanted to have their own dining room, to live with each other and, worse, to segregate themselves from white students.

This is exactly what we were trying not to do. We were trying to integrate blacks and whites, not have blacks as a separate group. The black demands on Colgate for this social separation became, as these things do in colleges, a major feud between the white and the black students and the administration.

Finally, for some reason I don't understand—I probably opened my mouth once too often in a board meeting—the president of the college asked me to come up and try to cope with what looked like a real revolution. I went and talked to the blacks and found out what their complaints were. I talked to the whites, found out what theirs were and came up with a reasonable compromise that calmed things down and got them going again.

I don't remember the details of the compromise, but I think a very large part of its success was just letting everyone blow off steam and making sure they knew I understood. It worked so well that the Colgate newspaper, the *Colgate Maroon*, wrote a long, very laudatory editorial saying, "Harvey Picker ought to be running this university because then we wouldn't have the problems we have." I was startled and very pleased.

From my experience, I've come to believe that the board of an academic institution has just one function: to see that they have an administration that's doing the job it ought to do, setting policy. The board should stay out of administration. Now that's not a very easy thing to do, but board members are not administrators, and they must be very careful to leave the administration to handle the actual operations.

[14]
Jean: Her Life

Jean had a chronic health problem that was like the sword of Damocles hanging over her. A fistula ran from under her left ear around her spine to her throat. She and I had been told it would kill her. It was the result of mastoiditis, an inflammation of the temporal bone behind the ear, that was not treated properly when she was a child as a result of her mother's refusal to allow her to be operated on. It threatened her throughout her lifetime.

Jean bore this burden with remarkable fortitude. The fistula would close up, and then it would become remarkably painful. Once when we were driving from Larchmont to New York City for a UN reception, it burst. Jean refused to go home; instead, she bought and put on some bandages. She wore them all the time. Instead of hiding the area under her hair, as most women would have done, she left it quite obviously exposed.

That's who Jean was. She never tried to hide this condition, and she carried on despite everything until there finally came a day when she had to have an operation because a brain abscess was forming.

The doctor who was treating her examined it and concluded that it had become much larger. He said that her condition had become very dangerous, and that Jean should be prepared to consider that she probably would not live a year. Imagine our reaction to this information. When Jean developed this brain abscess, it was decided to risk operating.

During the operation and for about three days afterward, Jean was fine. Then it developed that the left side of her face was getting paralyzed, and then her vocal chords were paralyzed. She had Bell's palsy, which couldn't be treated. And she couldn't talk because her vocal chords weren't working. This raised an important question: Jean had been a U.S. delegate to the UN since 1968; to do her job, she had to be able to talk.

Finally she got the diagnosis. Everything would be fine, but it would take quite a while. George H.W. Bush, now President, had been the head of the delegation Jean served. Jean told him she was resigning because she could no longer fill the post, and George's answer was, "You get better and come back, because I am holding your place until you do."

This was quite remarkable, because the President knew this was a position that others wanted. It certainly strengthened Jean's feeling that she must figure out how to get better. And she did.

A year and half later I had the tremendous thrill of going to New York and seeing Jean stand up and speak in front of the whole General Assembly. Part of the thrill was that I had been able to help her get there.

When Jean was first able to talk again, she spoke so softly that it was difficult to hear her even if you were sitting close to her. I discussed possibilities with the Picker engineers in the

Cleveland factory, where we'd been manufacturing lecterns with amplifiers in them so you could set one up in front of an audience and talk.

I told the engineers, "We've got to figure out how to make a very small portable device so that people can hear Jean talk." We developed something about the size of a woman's handbag to act as an amplifier. The microphone was a very thin wire that hung down from Jean's eyeglasses in front of her mouth. This miniature microphone had just been developed for use by astronauts, and the wire was barely noticeable. Jean could come into a room, put her handbag on the table and be heard by everyone.

Other people, seeing the device, asked where they could buy it. "I'm sorry," I said. "You can't."

And they said, "Well, we really want one."

And I said, "You probably couldn't buy it, because what it takes for purchase is an organization with a group of great engineers sitting down and working on this problem very seriously for quite a while."

Jean was immensely popular at the UN. She was there at a time when the United States and the Arab countries were in conflict, and anything the United States proposed in the UN was immediately vetoed by the Arab states. During a debate on a subject I don't remember, the delegate from Syria stood up in committee and launched a tirade against Jean, a personal attack that included a reference to the "Picker policy of deceit."

This kind of thing was not done at the UN. You didn't mention another person's name, and you never attacked anybody personally. The Arab countries held Jean in such high regard that when the vote was called, every Arab state except Syria voted in favor of the United States. After the vote, many delegates walked up to apologize to her.

Jean did a great deal behind the scenes at the UN. She and I were Quakers, and many of the foreign delegates trusted that the Quaker meeting house near the UN was not bugged. It was completely safe to discuss things that would not be leaked. A great many other countries were willing to meet and talk with Jean there.

Delegates were required to send a report of the day's meetings to the State Department every day, along with recommendations for what positions the United States should take. Sometimes a reception would go on and on, and Jean would work late into the night to file a report. (That's why we had an apartment very close to the UN.) And the next morning, before going to any meetings, she had to wait for instructions from the State Department. It was ludicrous, really, because she'd send her recommendations at night, and the next morning the State Department would send back its recommendations, which were her recommendations copied back to her. The people at the State Department had a great deal of respect for her.

Jean loved her work at the UN. She went on to serve as the special senior adviser to the delegations of six General Assemblies and to eight sessions of the Economic and Social Council under Presidents Nixon and Ford. In 1978 she was named the president of the United Nations Association of the United States of America, an independent group founded by Eleanor Roosevelt to educate others about the nature and function of the UN.

[15]

Jean and I

Although there were only three aspects of our lives that Jean and I regarded as joint projects—our daughters; the Picker Foundation, later Picker Institute, which we created in 1987; and cruising on *Branta*, the boat we had designed and built in 1968—there was between us a continuous interchange of ideas and efforts in support of each other's work.

One of these interchanges involved membership on the Council on Foreign Relations. In those days, the council was a small, exclusive and extremely prestigious all-male organization. I became a member in the late 1960s.

At about the same time, the council decided to join the increasingly popular trend to admit women. Because the membership was solely male, one of the problems that became immediately apparent was how to deal with the fact that every member would propose his wife for membership. That led, not surprisingly, to the decision that no wives of members would be eligible to join the council.

When President Johnson appointed Jean to the UN, a very prestigious post in foreign affairs, I decided that she shouldn't be denied membership because of me. I preferred to resign rather than block her membership, so I proposed that she replace me. The council considered the situation and decided that regardless of their policy, they'd retain me and elect Jean to membership.

It was very popular then to name women to the boards of large corporations. But they were added mostly for public relations purposes rather than as serious board members. That was not for Jean. At the time, she knew many women on the boards of U.S. companies. She was appalled to discover that many of these women couldn't understand corporate finance, although they were well known for their charitable work. She organized a group of women who were based in or near New York and said "Look, we sit there as figureheads because we don't understand the intricacies of accounting. So let's get some economists to educate us." This became a regular meeting of the women on the boards of major corporations to bring them up to speed.

The seminar was very effective, and Jean put what she learned to good use. She was the first woman appointed to the board of the Bank of Tokyo Trust Company, which was a lot larger than any American bank. And I think she was not only the first woman but also the first non-Japanese board member. Typical of Jean, she was very sensitive to Japanese custom. She never attended the lunch before the directors' meeting. She never spoke during a meeting but talked to the chairman afterward about her reactions. She was very discreet in handling this type of situation.

Also typical of Jean were her actions as a member of the bank's audit committee. Handed a set of papers to sign, she saw that it included a notice from the bank to the audit company saying that she, on the bank's behalf, had given the audit company all the information it needed, that the information was accurate and that therefore she had disclosed to the audit company everything that needed to be disclosed.

Jean looked at the document and said, "But I haven't. I don't even know what's in the books. I can't sign this." So they patiently explained to this dumb woman that this was done every year and had been done every year for years. And none of the others knew any more about it than she did.

And Jean said, "You know I haven't had the books. I haven't read them and I haven't handed them to you." And they, still patient, explained that she had to do this because the auditors wouldn't work without the signed notice. And Jean just as patiently explained that she needed proof.

So the auditors came in and explained exactly what she wanted to know, though I gather that this system of signing without reading has persisted to this day.

I suspect there were executives in the bank's financial department, as well as among the auditors, who would cheerfully have assassinated Jean. It was typical of her that she was not overawed by this, or by anything else.

One of the sidelights of Jean's term on the bank's board turned out to be very valuable for me. Jean was invited to Tokyo with the rest of the board. The Japanese had arranged appropriate entertainment for the spouses of the board members, and I had the choice of going to the tea ceremony or learning to arrange flowers. I was appreciative, I told them, but I wasn't going to do either. So I made an appointment to see a friend of mine, Dr. Kiichiro Toyoda, who in 1937 had founded an automobile company as a spin-off from his family's company, Toyota Industries. I knew Dr. Toyoda because, unlike any other company directors I knew, Dr. Toyoda and his top executives came to Columbia each year to get a briefing on the United States and what it was doing and where it was heading, and on our views about other countries.

When I got to the Toyota plant, Dr. Toyoda came out to meet me. I had noticed an extra flag on the flagpole and asked him what it was. "The Deming Award," he said. I congratulated him on this distinction. Later I asked him about a button he was wearing on his lapel, and he said, "That's the personal Deming Award."

I happened to know what the Deming Award was, but when I came back to the United States and talked with people about this visit, I never ran into anybody who knew what the award was. Dr. W. Edwards Deming was an American and the person who had written the basic book on quality control. The award was for outstanding quality control. American companies didn't know Deming existed. Now they do. But it was typical of Toyota that the company had invested in quality control at the time that people thought stuff from Japan was junk.

I went through the Toyota factory. Unlike what others had told me about Japanese production systems, it was an old-fashioned plant. There was nothing in it that looked like a modern gadget at all. I asked Dr. Toyoda, "I notice that these cars are being taken off the production line and set aside. What goes on?" He said, "Everybody working on the production line is responsible for seeing that the car doesn't have any defects. If it has any defect at all, no matter what the worker's task is, he raises his hand, and that car is taken off the line. It doesn't matter if it affects his job or anybody else's. The car just gets taken off the line, the defect is made good and then it's put back on."

How much more sensible this was than the American system of completing the car, finding the defect—if you find it—in the inspection department and then taking the car apart again to fix the defect! It was true that the Toyota system slowed the production line, but it lowered the overall cost of quality control if you did quality control at every step of the way. I'm interested to see that this is now playing out in many ways. Many Japanese cars, including Toyotas, are regarded as being more reliable than American cars. And Americans, as far as I can see, don't do much research into what the rest of the world is doing and worry about it, as we saw Toyota do.

[16]

Travels Together

Jean and I were so heavily involved in our jobs that we took great delight in experiencing new aspects of life, when we were able, with each other and with our daughters. This led to our custom of planning very early in the year where we wanted to travel the next year and making arrangements to do so.

When our daughters were in their early teens, we decided that scenery and wildlife, both at sea and on land, would provide them with a good outdoor education. We booked two cabins on one of the popular Alaska transport system ferries. There were no roads leading to the cities in southern Alaska, so that all transport (except airplanes) was by trucks, people and automobiles loaded on these ferries.

Accommodations are quite simple. But on the top deck of the ferry you can find space reserved for those who want to "camp out." That meant putting up your tent in a sheltered area, securing it to the deck and living exactly as though you were camping ashore. The ferries also boasted very informal dining rooms and even tiny cabins.

We went to Ivujivik, the northernmost Inuit village in Alaska. Because of the permafrost and the sled dogs, the smell was frightful. The leading characteristics of those lovable sled dogs you see in Disney DVDs is that they are nasty and you don't want to get at all close to one.

As it turned out, I believe that the ship's crew provided most of the education for Bobbi and Gale on the trip. Obviously they had reached the age when every minute they had free was spent in the crew's quarters. (No, not doing anything that would be regarded as wrong, but being intrigued by these creatures who looked like humans but wore pants!)

Yet we did see wonderful wildlife—whales, orcas, reindeer—as well as glaciers, beautiful waterfalls and fascinating villages populated by the Inuit and white settlers.

Another trip was far more interesting. A year or two after the end of World War II, while attending an international exhibit of X-ray apparatus, I began to think that Japan would, in the foreseeable future, develop into a sizeable market for Picker equipment.

Therefore, having obtained a reasonable education in Japanese customs, business practice and courtesy, Jean and I set off for Tokyo, where a relatively small company named Kishimoto had attracted my attention.

I knew that in Japan at that time, if a businessman interested in working with a Japanese company was accompanied by an attorney, the Japanese reaction was quite apt to be: "What is the matter with him? He doesn't even know his own business well enough to discuss it and come to an agreement."

The custom was for the two CEOs to travel together long enough to decide whether they trusted each other and whether they had enough interests in common to make some sort of a partnership desirable.

We were met at the plane by Kim Kishimoto, the CEO of Kishimoto, and, since Jean was accompanying me, his wife. Both Kim and his wife understood and spoke English easily, were most accommodating and were not only delightful but extremely interesting people.

We toured much of Japan in their car, and some fascinating questions arose in the course of our conversations. Two examples: "My wife holds my overcoat for me. Why do you hold her overcoat for your wife?"

And then the second question that we found very intriguing: "Almost all of us believe in two religions. We are married in a Shinto shrine and buried in a Buddhist ceremony. In addition to these two religions, a very large part of our population also includes Christianity in their beliefs. Why do Americans believe that you must not belong to two different religions? In fact, you may not even belong simultaneously to two aspects of Christianity, such as Congregational and Episcopal."

As a clear signal that we had proven acceptable, our tour ended at the home of Kim's uncle, a lovely, large house and grounds outside Tokyo. Kim had been adopted by his uncle so that Kim could be CEO of the company.

Kim's uncle was dressed as an English golfer would be, and when Jean complimented him on the tea we were served, he replied, "I'm glad you like it. It is Twining's."

A real problem arose when Kim and his uncle took us through the house and the uncle presented us with a beautiful inlaid box that for generations had contained the sewing kit for the christening clothes for the firstborn in the family.

Not surprisingly, Jean and I found this overly generous. Jean expressed that sentiment, and we got ourselves in a mess. Our hosts took Jean's reluctance to mean that the gift was not good enough, and we spent the rest of the afternoon trying to maneuver ourselves back to the sewing kit. Finally we succeeded, and to this day it stands exhibited in the hallway of my house.

Our lives continued to be interlinked with the Kishimotos for many years. Kim's sister came to the United States to study. She fell in love with her music teacher and married him. As a result, she was immediately disowned and disinherited by her family, leaving her without money or friends. We helped her through that period while trying to persuade the Kishimoto family to reconsider. They eventually did, but it took at least five years.

Picker and Kishimoto worked together very successfully for several years until the rapid growth of the Japanese X-ray manufacturing industry eliminated imports.

Another venturesome trip was our circumnavigation of South America. This was before the days of jets and pressurized planes. Flights took a long time, and heading for high altitude in the Andes meant you were handed a tube with branches to provide oxygen to every passenger. As Jean pointed out, it was something less than hygienic because it allowed everyone's saliva to mix with that of those in nearby seats. We learned much about Peru, which at the time was largely influenced by the Japanese. We took the obligatory trip to Machu Pichu where I promptly, due to my own stupidity, developed altitude sickness.

Returning to the lowlands, we went on to Chile to go skiing in the Andes. To reach the one ski area in the country at the time, we went to the train station. Our "train" proved to be an old Ford with automobile wheels replaced by railroad wheels.

No one had bothered to grade the single track that ran over the mountain range from Santiago to Buenos Aires. At times it climbed at an alarming angle, then descended at an even scarier angle. If one thought that any power was apt to pay attention, prayer would be very useful.

Since there were no signals on the single track, traffic was "self-controlled." Every 15 or 20 miles there was a small shack alongside the track. If it contained the appropriate flag, the driver left the one he had, took the new one and went ahead to the next stop. He evidently had faith in the system. We were dubious, but we had no choice.

At about nightfall we arrived at our destination, a small inn at the foot of an open, snow-covered slope. The next morning we discovered that the slope and the lift left something to be desired.

The slope was large and steep but had the unusual characteristic of ending in a deep mountain lake without having any flat, or almost flat, runout at the bottom. The lift chairs had no armrests to keep one from falling off the side, nor did they have any seat belts. Hence riding up the lift was as much of an adventure as skiing down the slope. It appeared that the two of us were the entire guest population at the resort, so at least we didn't have to worry about other skiers. Somehow or other we subsequently passed up any opportunity to go back there.

From there we continued on the single track, but this time in a real train. Arriving in Buenos Aires at nightfall, we had the experience of sleeping in a very nice hotel on the town square. These were the days of Juan Perón, and we awoke in the morning thinking we had somehow been transported to Germany. Goose-stepping troops singing German-sounding songs were parading around the square.

Buenos Aires was lovely, but there was no doubt that the government was as close to a Nazi regime as one could find outside of the real thing.

Jean and I decided we'd better be careful about where we went and what we said. We found the Argentinean "asado" a delightful outdoor dining experience but were glad to leave the country for Rio.

Our next stop was the Amazon. We were to be the guests of the Brazilian Public Health Agency to observe the methods used to help improve the life and life expectancy of the natives who lived in the jungle beside the river.

The city of Manaus is the capital of Amazonas State, in northwest Brazil. The flight from Rio to Manaus is very long indeed, especially in a propeller plane. Manaus is a large, modern city. The Teatro Amazonas, an opera house built in 1896, is a notable landmark, reflecting the massive wealth of the turn-of-the-century rubber boom. During its heyday, some of the finest singers in the world performed there.

Setting out on our inspection tour, we boarded a 35-foot motorboat, accompanied by a pilot and a public health physician and nurse, as well as a deckhand/cook.

There's no need to tell you that the Amazon is huge. Even on a clear day you can't see the opposite shore. The river is full of deadly fish that sting or bite, and navigating requires skill and experience to avoid going aground or hitting dangerous debris. The jungle is so dense, right down to the water, that even if you were able to swim ashore, I doubt whether you could make your way to dry land.

It is also hot and humid—much worse than the New York subway on a day in August!

We cruised upstream until the pilot found a place for us to come ashore at something that looked like a dock put together by someone who had heard of such a thing but never seen one. Almost instantaneously a group of natives gathered at the shore to watch us. They sat down at the dock, and it soon became clear that we were, as far as they were concerned, the greatest entertainment around.

We were taken on a short tour of the town. It couldn't be anything but short. There were no more than about a dozen grass huts.

The public health nurse showed us the latest gift to the town, of which the townsfolk around us were clearly proud. It was a large concrete slab, about eight by ten feet, with a large oval hole in it. Obviously, with a hole dug under it, it was the community bathroom.

We strolled back to the boat and had a simple dinner, but none of our dockside audience departed. Indeed, they stayed motionless on the dock, watching us even as we prepared to climb into our berths and went to sleep. When we awoke the next morning, not a one seemed to have lost interest.

I guess for the amusement of the audience, at breakfast the cook gave me a fruit to taste that so puckered my mouth I couldn't even open it to talk. Our audience appreciated the entertainment.

Then the nurse and the doctor explained the health system: Since there weren't enough public health personnel, or good enough communications, to scatter them among the tiny villages and be at all effective, the public health system had turned to "witch" doctors for help.

First, the witch doctors were brought together to hear how important they were. Then they were told that they were to become even more important. Each was given a silver badge and a large leather physician's bag that contained packets of white powder that only they would have. When a baby was born, they were to use the white powder instead of animal dung to stop the bleeding at the umbilical cord. When they needed more white powder, they sent a messenger, and the packets would be replaced as long as the messenger brought the list of the babies born, including their sex and where and when the child was born.

Furthermore, these jungle doctors now had the power to call a public health doctor if the delivery was not going well, or if a person had been badly injured. In that case, they were to send the silver badge to the nearest station and a doctor would be immediately dispatched to assist.

From what Jean and I could see, it was an ingenious and effective system—much better than trying to eliminate the witch doctors, as was more commonly done in other developing countries.

Our voyage ended at Belém, another cosmopolitan city in the jungle that was a memorial to the great importance of rubber until substitutes were discovered.

The length of the flight back to Rio was emphasized when we ran out of reading matter. The kind stewardess offered us magazines, but neither Jean nor I could read Portuguese. She then offered us a deck of cards, but at that point we both discovered that neither of us had much of an idea about card games beyond the childish ones such as Slap-Jack. It was indeed a long trip back to Rio.

It was in the 1950s, during my term on the board of directors of an organization called the African Medical Research Foundation, that Jean and I visited Kenya. The foundation's mission was to find ways to improve healthcare for the native Kenyans who still lived in the bush in fairly primitive conditions.

We were trying to develop a low-cost, pragmatic method to reduce deaths from malaria in the small tribal villages. Part of the program involved a small team of healthcare professionals who traveled in a large van in the bush in Kenya and in what is now Tanzania. The objective was to teach the nomadic tribes enough simple hygiene to increase their life expectancy, even if only a little. But it appeared to us on the board that the van was doing very little. I was asked to go to Kenya and find out why the program wasn't being more active.

Jean and I went to Kenya and found the van. A picture of Jean up to her waist in a muddy river, trying to help a group of stalwart natives push the van out of the river, provided a vivid example of why the van couldn't go very far.

Another method we tried was showing movies on a large screen outside the van to attract the natives and help them understand the need to use netting to reduce fly and mosquito bites. After a screening, I asked one of the natives who spoke English what he thought of the show. He said that it was interesting but that it didn't apply to his people.

"Why not?" I asked.

He replied that there weren't any such huge flies or mosquitoes in his area as were depicted on the movie screen.

Before we left for Kenya, I'd said to Jean that it seemed a shame that we were to go to the finest place in the world to go on a safari—to be right in safari country and not enjoy the safari experience. As I should have expected, a couple of weeks later, Jean told me that we had a safari in the bush all laid on for our next vacation.

Neither Jean nor I had ever shot anything except clay pigeons, but we were instructed to bring our own guns and ammunition. We also had to decide on what caliber and type of gun we wanted, and to choose between iron sights or telescopic sights. And we certainly didn't realize that the guns had to be fitted to us.

All this led to a great amount of research and confusion, because no matter what book you read, some other book disagreed. However, when we finally boarded our plane to Africa, we were carrying guns that we hoped were acceptable. A remarkably handsome guide met us at the plane and took us to the hotel. Then he set about seeing that proper bush clothing was made for us overnight and took us to have our guns registered with the authorities.

Our trip was during the Mau Mau uprising, a revolt by Kenyan rebels from 1952 to 1960 against British colonialist rule that was to set the stage for Kenyan independence in 1963. Quite a few natives and British had already been killed. The police made it quite clear that our guns were not to stray, and that if we returned without a gun, we could expect to experience living in jail in their country for quite some time.

As I said, neither Jean nor I had ever shot anything in our lives, and we had no intention of starting now. But our guide explained to us that the sixteen natives who were accompanying us were paid fifty cents a day and expected to get meat, because otherwise they would eat just potatoes and vegetables. They wanted meat not only for themselves but to take home to their families.

I said to the guide, "Fine. You shoot it and we'll eat it." And he said, "No, my job is to find the game for you, and you shoot it." And you can do it, if you hunt carefully.

I think people who wind up killing another hunter should go to prison for murder. If you're going to shoot an animal, you'd better not shoot it just because it's "there." You go through all the effort of stalking it until you can see exactly what part of the animal you want to hit. And you don't just shoot at an animal: You know what you're aiming for. We didn't shoot anything except for the meat; we didn't shoot animals for trophies.

I did come back with a trophy, however. Early one morning we decided to cross a field, and one of the big rocks in the field started to move. On closer examination, it turned out to be a rhinoceros. And the rhinoceros didn't like me. I didn't think much of it either, I have to say. But it started at me and—well, a rhino can move faster than a horse. So I shot it. I was close enough to see that the bullet hit the heart and went inside at exactly the right place. But the rhino just kept accelerating, so I shot it again, and again I hit the heart. That didn't faze the rhino either. It just kept coming. I don't think my next two shots were as accurate. But the rhino came thundering at me and passed to one side—about twenty feet away, very near me—and took a few more steps and dropped dead.

I don't like rhinos, and apparently they don't like me.

That wasn't the end of it. We used the carcass to try to catch a leopard that had killed a couple of children from a nearby village.

In 1983, NATO invited Jean and me on an inspection tour. We were graciously received at NATO headquarter and briefed on its mission and the difficulty of carrying it out. From NATO headquarters in Belgium we were taken to the American tank division stationed at the border opposite the Fulda Gap, a region between the East German border and Frankfurt. This part of the frontier had been used for centuries by troops from either east or west to invade the other side, and during the Cold War it was strategically important. The commander of the NATO division made no attempt to hide his concern that the American tanks were no match for the new Soviet tanks, and that were an invasion to be attempted, his sector would almost certainly be overrun by the new, larger, better-armored Soviet model.

From Germany we were taken to Naples and onto a large U.S naval vessel. At sea, we were briefed by a young naval officer on the problems NATO faced in the Mediterranean. He attributed a large part of the difficulty to the volatile young population in the Muslim countries, including many extremists. The civil war in Lebanon was taking place at the time, and NATO's mission was, insofar as possible, that of peacekeeper.

The officer proudly explained to us that the day before, the Christian troops had been pinned against the coast and had run out of ammunition. The U.S. fleet had laid down a curtain of fire that protected the Christian troops until they could be supplied with ammunition by their own forces.

On hearing the news, far from applauding it, I turned to Jean and said, "Now the United States is in real trouble. That action has moved us from being a peacekeeping force to being combatants."

A few weeks later, on Oct. 23, 1983, when a terrorist exploded a truck bomb at the entrance to the Marine barracks, killing 241 servicemen, the United States reacted as though this were an unprovoked attack.

[17]
In the Soviet Union

At the end of World War II, the United States and the Soviet Union, though not technically at war, actually were at war. The Soviet Union was diligently and effectively converting to communism countries from Cuba to East Germany and Vietnam. The United States, while avoiding direct confrontation, did much to support and even arm countries that were seen as vulnerable to Soviet suasion.

Partly as a result of U.S. Senator Joseph McCarthy's hysterical, and very successful, tactics, the United States suspected that the Soviet Union was even subverting this country to communism. Beginning in 1950, many of America's "best and brightest" had their careers blighted or destroyed by McCarthy's unsupported accusations of being communist sympathizers. McCarthy was so effective that even President Eisenhower repeatedly did his bidding. A large part of the American public was demonstrating something very like mass hysteria over the so-called red menace.

Others, including many of Jean's colleagues at the UN, rather than growing hysterical, seriously labored to convince potential future leaders in the developing countries of the advantages of democracy and capitalism.

But there was no mistaking the antipathy between the United States and the Soviet Union. Germany provided a good example. At the end of the war, Germany was to be ruled by the four victors. But the Soviet Union, declaring that East Germany was Soviet territory, extended its border to include that area, even fortifying the border against incursions from the West or escapes of Germans to the West.

In 1956, in reply to what had become Jean's annual question about where to go for our next winter trip, and knowing it was closed to U.S. tourists, I, half in earnest and half in jest, suggested the Soviet Union. Jean took me seriously and applied for a visa. To our surprise, it was granted about six months later. It specified the organization, Intourist, that we were to use as a travel agent and that we were to enter the Soviet Union from Finland on January 2 on a certain scheduled flight.

As she always did when going to a strange place, Jean asked the State Department about traveling as a visitor to the Soviet Union. What had been the experience of others? The reply from the State Department was that there was no such thing. No U.S. visitors were being admitted.

When Jean said she had the visas in her hand, the people at State were astounded. Their advice was: "Remember, you will be on your own. We cannot help you. If you can arrange it, try to leave from Moscow so our embassy can tell whether you've been released."

We dutifully went to Helsinki at the end of December. Here we experienced a genuine sauna during which an unusually large and powerful woman who spoke no English took charge of us. She handled us as she might a couple of pancakes on a griddle and offered us the full program, including rolling in the snow in sub-zero temperatures and being beaten with birch branches. Jean and I most reluctantly declined the two add-ons. However, we did survive the rest of the experience and made it to the plane the next day.

We were met at the Moscow airport by our Intourist escort, an attractive young woman who spoke English well. She answered the simple questions such as identifying buildings and other places of interest. but she avoided answering questions that had any political implications whatsoever. After we checked in at the Intourist office at our hotel, we soon had our room keys and the opportunity to unpack and lie down.

There was little or no effort to hide the fact that we were being watched all the time. Conversations in our room were monitored, and our luggage was searched when we were out of our room. We'd anticipated this, so it didn't bother us.

Moscow was a fairly clean, well-lit city. We were free to walk wherever we wished. On our first night there we got tickets to the ballet. We were tremendously impressed with the dance presentation, as we were with the care and maintenance that had gone into the very elegant cultural buildings from the tsarist days.

Service in the dining room was good. The food was not at all European but distinctly Russian, nourishing and somewhat monotonous but tasty and well-cooked. There was, however, an undertone that made us feel as though the people who were serving us felt quite superior to us.

The next morning, we were greeted at the Intourist office by a new guide, a woman a little older than the one who had met us at the airport. The Intourist people courteously inquired what we wanted to see, and after some discussion we agreed to a schedule.

At this time Jean was a volunteer lecturer with the UN's Office of Public Information, engaged in disseminating information and education, and in the course of the discussion, she made it quite clear that she wanted to visit the UN's library in Moscow.

She got no response to her suggestion, so each morning thereafter, with increasing emphasis, she reiterated the request. Each time it was put off for the future. Frustrated, Jean finally became so forceful that I had vivid visions of the huge gates of KGB headquarters, the infamous Lubyanka prison, closing behind us. Jean finally declared that unless she was taken to see the library the next day, we were going home. At that point a higher Intourist official came in and explained that the library was closed tomorrow but would be available the morning after.

Taking him at his word, Jean agreed to stay. The morning of the second day, a different guide took us to what looked like an upper-class apartment building. There were no signs outside the building or the large, well-lit apartment we were taken to. Inside, there were a large number of glass cases containing opened books.

When Jean asked why all the books were in English when Russian editions were available, she was told that the Russian translations were so bad that more Soviet people were able to read the English. Jean mildly pointed out that that was strange, since it was the Soviet government that selected the translator.

We wandered around the apartment for more than an hour. In all that time, no one else appeared. We then returned to the car and went on with our sightseeing.

What had we actually seen? You should know that at that time the UN was paying the Soviet Union a monthly fee for maintaining a library in Moscow as well as paying for the translator and the entire operation.

Although we did not comment any further, it was pretty obvious that what we had seen was a "Potemkin village," not an operating library. Evidently the Soviets, short on foreign currency, wanted the United States to continue paying for a library that didn't exist. They had hoped to mislead Jean, who had to report to the UN office for which she worked.

A similar thing occurred when we visited the Hermitage, the beautiful former Winter Palace, now a museum in Leningrad. On exhibit were paintings that would be envied by any museum in the world. There were, however, no paintings done after the Russian Revolution. Quiet inquiry revealed that, yes, their collection included many of the finest works of the modernists, but they were carefully preserved and sequestered in the basement.

During our trip we saw that the Soviet healthcare system was still using a large number of Picker X-ray field units, and much other equipment that was not of recent design. Healthcare was available without charge to everyone. In fact, it was illegal to pay for services, but we discovered that it was a widespread custom for physicians to go home in mid-afternoon, when "friends" would stop in to chat, politely leaving a little memento when they departed.

Besides keeping national treasures intact, be they pre-revolutionary palaces and museums or of more recent construction, I was impressed that much of the Soviet technology was as advanced as ours.

We visited the U.S. embassy often. We, and the staff, soon discovered that we knew much more about what was going on in the country at the time than the embassy did. The Soviets had placed restrictions on all visitors, but they gave us much greater freedom to travel, inspect and see aspects of the country than was available to embassy personnel.

After we returned home, I discussed our trip on numerous speaking engagements, and I learned that my evaluation of Soviet technological advances was causing the McCarthy forces to question my patriotism. Fortunately for me, the Soviet Union deployed Sputnik later that year, on Oct. 4, 1957, making me look like a wise man instead of a fellow traveler.

I'm not certain what put us in the Soviets' good graces, but we were given ready admission to all but the most restricted places. In 1983, when I retired as dean at Columbia's School of International Affairs, the Soviets invited Jean and me to visit their country as their guests. They asked me where I wanted to go. Taking advantage of the blank check, I asked to visit Akadem Gorodok, a highly restricted "academic town " where much research was carried on, outside Novosibirsk in western Siberia.

To my great surprise, my request was granted. Memorable during that visit was the opportunity I had to chat with one of the Soviet Union's leading economists. I'd been told by knowledgeable American economists that the Soviets would never be able to organize their economy effectively because they had not discovered the analytic system we in the United States used then to determine the health of the marketplace. To my surprise, talking with that Soviet economist revealed that not only was he, and other economists in his country, aware of the system, but that he had used it to analyze both the Soviet and the United States economies.

Over the years, by the way, I've learned that the United States has an inherent belief that its own exceptionalism makes it superior to any other country. I can't resist pointing out, however, that part of my officer education by the Navy in the period just before Pearl Harbor included a series of lectures assuring us that our fleet was completely safe in Pearl Harbor. There was no way the Japanese could damage it. Nor, for that matter, could they attack Clark Air Base on Luzon Island, or the Bataan Peninsula, in the Philippines. I only wish our instructors could have convinced the Japanese that this American gospel was true.

But to return to the Soviet Union. Eleanor Roosevelt had been invited back to the Soviet Union on the tenth anniversary of the

Yalta Conference, where President Roosevelt, Winston Churchill and Joseph Stalin decided on the fate of Europe after the war. On her return to the United States, Eleanor came to our home for dinner and talked about her experience. She spoke of how kind the Soviets were to her and mentioned that they had even brought the translator who had been assigned to Roosevelt at Yalta out of retirement to take care of her.

"Was that translator Anna Lavrovna?" I asked.

Mrs. Roosevelt, quite surprised, answered, "Yes. How did you know?"

I had guessed, because Anna Lavrovna was the mature woman who had very quickly replaced our young tour guide on our first visit to the Soviet Union.

[18]
Teaching at Colgate

In 1970, the dean of faculty of Colgate University invited me to take on a part-time teaching job. I thought this was a great opportunity. After all, if you're studying to be a plumber, you ought to get a chance to see what it's like to be a plumber and find out if you really want to go through with it. So I accepted a position as an adjunct faculty member at Colgate.

I drove to Colgate, which is in Hamilton, New York, near Syracuse, every Sunday night and taught a seminar Monday evening. Eventually, flouting all the protocols of teaching, I started inviting a different professor to each session to critique my teaching technique. In a college or graduate school, it's unusual for a member of the faculty or the administration to come to your class unless he or she has been invited as a guest lecturer, but I learned a lot from these professors, and I discovered that I liked teaching.

Harvey liked and admired strong women, of whom his wife, Jean, was a perfect example. Photograph by Arnold Newman

I'd been teaching for about a year. I'd gotten all the course credits I needed to get my Ph.D., but I hadn't yet written my thesis, when Colgate invited me to take on the serious task of being part of its faculty. That was very valuable and enabled me to learn a lot more.

At the time, Colgate offered a set of survey courses that students were required to take. The classes were team-taught by a group of professors, and I was asked to teach on a team. This gave me a wonderful advantage, because we met each week to discuss the results of the previous session and how we would teach the next session. To be able to analyze what you're teaching and how to do it really brought me along as a person who was learning what he needed to know.

One of the ludicrous things about the situation was that occasionally Jean would go from all the panoply and formal affairs that went with her position at the UN, being well-known in international circles and treated as a VIP, to Colgate, with me, where we had been given two rooms in the men's dormitory. We cooked on an electric stove on top of the refrigerator. Sometimes we'd invite other faculty members for meals, and they always exclaimed what a good cook Jean was and ask her for her recipes. Of course, we'd brought the meals up from various very good caterers in the New York area, and Jean just warmed them up.

She also did the laundry, and she was a little bit shocked at doing it while very good-looking young men roamed around without any clothes on. It was completely different from what she was used to, and she took it all as great sport. Instead of saying, as you might expect, "Look, I like being a VIP better than being a faculty member's wife," she played her part gladly, and enjoyed it. This was typical of the way Jean encouraged and supported me in my work.

I've been fortunate in having strong, accomplished women in my life. When you're married to someone like Jean, who is competent and has excellent judgment, you have somebody to discuss ideas with. You have a good way of measuring yourself, knowing whether you're doing things right or not.

I was always able to go to Jean and my mother and sister for advice—or to my father, in regard to business. When these people all leave you, the difference is tremendous. Not being able to discuss issues with somebody you know will be on your side but will also serve you objectively makes you less and less certain about your judgment. Indeed, one of my problems today is that I have no way to make that measurement.

In my life, I have always found inspiration in women who are accomplished and well informed. Anyone who says half the human race isn't as smart and as competent and as important as the other half is crazy.

[19]

Graduate School of International Affairs

In 1972, while I was teaching at Colgate, my thesis advisor, Bill Fox, the same well-known scholar who had been on the board of the Hudson Institute and gotten me into Columbia, called me one day and said, "The dean of the Graduate School of International Affairs is retiring, and I'd like to propose you as his successor."

I said the obvious. "Bill, you're kidding. I don't even have my Ph.D., and you can get a very distinguished diplomat like the one you have who is retiring or an outstanding scholar for this post. There's no point in putting my name in." But Bill insisted, and finally I said, "Bill, I understand how these things work. You want to prove you've made a thorough search, so you'll have a lot of names that you can cross off as soon as you put them down.

Put mine down if you want." Then I pretty much dismissed it from my mind.

About four months later, I got a call from the secretary of the president of the university, Bill McGill, asking me to come see him. I allowed that I was pretty busy but that I could probably get around to see him in another month or so. When I did finally get to see him, we chatted for a little bit and then he said he'd like me to take on the job of being the dean of the School of International Affairs. I said to him, as I had to Bill Fox, "Look, I don't have a Ph.D. I'm not a distinguished scholar, I'm not a distinguished diplomat. Why do you want me?"

Bill's answer was one I've always treasured: "I haven't got a clue. But the faculty wants you, and if you'll take the job, it'll be a lot easier for me."

In fact, Bill appeared to have thought well of me too. In an article in the *New York Times* he described me as "an extraordinary man, an administrator of unquestioned ability, an acknowledged expert on the relations between science, technology and government and a public servant whose activities on behalf of a better world indicate human qualities that are extremely precious."

In fact, I was delighted to take the post. After all, I was skipping a lot of years of being a junior faculty member. I didn't take the job at the time it was offered, but I went home and discussed it with Jean, and as I recall she offered to murder me if I didn't accept.

I realize, in retrospect, why the faculty wanted me. One, they knew me very well because I had been a student in their classes. Two, Bill Fox was very, very influential as a faculty member, and he probably maneuvered it so that I got the job.

If I was successful at that job, it was because I had guidance from Bill Fox. He lived in Connecticut, and I drove him home at least twice a week. I discussed what was going on and got his advice. He was an expert and highly respected, and he had great insights.

After I had been there about three years, I said to Bill, "What am I doing wrong? When I first called faculty meetings, the room was absolutely packed. Now I can't even get the faculty to come to meetings by offering them coffee and doughnuts."

Bill's answer was that during the first few years the faculty members were trying to decide whether I was the man for the job. Once they were satisfied that I was doing a good job, they didn't want to waste time on administration. They had other things to do. They were confident that I would do a fine job for them.

I actually did very little but learn for the first two years. Then I started to wonder why we had the curriculum we did and why some courses were required of the students and others not. So I applied to the Ford Foundation for a grant to study what courses a student in international affairs should take.

A month or two later I was invited over to the Ford Foundation, where I got one of the most astonishing offers I've ever had. They said they wouldn't give me the grant I'd applied for, which was no surprise. But then they said, "We'll give you a much larger grant, if you'll take it on. We don't think any of the deans of these schools really knows the answer to the questions you're raising. If you'll take half a dozen more deans and form a study group to decide what ought to be taught, we'll provide the funding.

I said, "Which deans do you want?"

They said, "You pick them."

You've got to admit that that's startling: to go in and get told they'll give you a lot more money than you asked for. The study turned out to be invaluable. I think the discussions that I and the other deans had while we worked with the Ford Foundation grant had a real impact on each of these deans. We all worked simultaneously, and we reached just about the same conclusions. I never actually followed it up, but I'm quite certain that most of them saw it, as I did, as a chance to get a new perspective on what we were doing.

At Columbia, at the time, the courses required of, or just offered to, the students were those the faculty thought they ought to offer or teach. And each faculty member felt that the most important thing for the students was to learn what he or she was teaching, whatever it was.

In my view, we were a trade school: We trained people for jobs. What jobs are out there that we should be training them for, and what are the requirements for those jobs?

As we researched that, we made many very interesting discoveries. A lot of our students wanted a government job. Most of them were headed for the State Department, but the State Department wasn't much interested in them. It wanted people who had attended the foreign service school. In addition, the State Department hired very few new people each year.

What branch of the government is most interested in people who know something about international affairs? I wouldn't have guessed it in years. It proved to be the Department of Agriculture. It's the largest exporting organization in the United States, so there were lots of jobs, but they had different requirements.

Another important thing was international finance. The school did nothing to teach economics and finance, and I argued to the faculty that you cannot teach international affairs without teaching economics, since most diplomacy, and most international affairs, have a financial basis. Everything goes back to money.

This was in 1973, at the time of the OPEC oil crisis, when the OPEC nations were making tremendous amounts of money, then sending that money to U.S. banks to reinvest it and safeguard their gains. U.S. banks were hard put to find a way of investing the money usefully. Now that they'd supported everything they could in the United States, they needed to send large amounts of the remaining money overseas.

It seemed like a fine idea for our students to advise on investing, and I set out to develop a curriculum that would help achieve this. But I discovered that the students who took these courses were having a hard time getting a job. Citibank, for example, hired people with a straight business school background. So I went to the president of Citibank and said, "Look, the people you're hiring know finance, but they don't know anything about your clients. Our students understand the political risk that a foreign loan can pose. They understand finance. They've taken courses in the business school. Why don't you take a couple of these students and see how they compare with the business school students?"

As a result, within a few years a great many of our students were heading for a career they'd never considered. If they had wanted a career in finance, they'd have gone to business school. And they hadn't gone to business school.

I said to the students, "Here's the opportunity of a lifetime. You can get a job immediately on graduation, and you can influence international affairs. In fact, it's the largest field in which you can get jobs right now." They flocked to international banking, and it benefited both the students and the people who hired them. In fact, within two years we could tell students that they had a better chance of getting a job in international banking if they came to the school of international affairs than if they went to the business school. And that's a pretty good record, because with the assurance of a job in a field that students liked, applications to the school skyrocketed.

The next year, I felt that we had to add another course as a requirement: statistics. When somebody gives you an economic analysis, you have to know whether the figures are based on a chi-squared or a regression analysis. Otherwise, you may be very misled.

At that point the faculty rebelled. They said I'd put in enough required courses and that this was way out of our field. It was their decision to make, and I didn't argue. But I explained to the students in the next incoming class why they ought to take a course in statistics, and 85 percent of the class took statistics that year. Seeing what happened, the faculty decided this ought to be a required course.

What is interesting about this, as I look back, is that if statistics had been an undergraduate course at Columbia, I'd have had no success at persuading the students. But graduate students are so goal-oriented that if somebody convinces them that they ought to do something they dislike because it will help their careers, they'll do it.

That's one of the big differences between graduate and undergraduate students. Undergraduates look at you with the attitude of Okay, I'm here, now convince me I ought to be taking this course. Graduate students think, I'm here, and I really don't like this subject, but how do I learn more about it? It's a very different attitude.

Concurrently, there was a problem with the faculty. Then, as now, Columbia had a magnificent faculty. Most members have enviable reputations and are the leaders in their field. Because of their intellectual capabilities and insights, they are an absolute joy to talk to and be with, and one of the great pleasures of my job was working with people who were so bright and curious and effective.

I found, however, that the economics courses that were being taught were of no use to our students. The economics department was primarily interested in advanced research, not in the nitty-gritty of what makes things work.

Another good example was Spanish. Columbia had a marvelous language department where Spanish was taught. I had instituted a program of sending students overseas for summer jobs where they worked for banks and companies, and I got reports back on what their employers thought of them and how well we'd taught them. I remember a report on a student who had gone to Spain and found great difficulty in working there. Why? Because the Spanish that he had learned at Columbia was the classical Spanish of the golden age of Cervantes, and that wasn't what banking was about now.

The same was true in a report from Germany that came back saying, We found Mr. Jones to be a very bright man and very anxious to help, but his knowledge of banking German is insufficient for him to do this job. As can happen in a graduate school when you're using a graduate arts and sciences faculty, the faculty were outstanding in their field, but they weren't teaching what our students needed to know. Nor were they about to change their career or sacrifice their position or prestige to go back to something that was not as highly regarded academically. The solution was to bring in adjunct faculty, people who were actually working in the field, who wanted to teach and who were willing to take a non-tenured position for a year or two.

We recruited more and more adjunct faculty so students could be aware of what was actually going on in those fields. I used to say to incoming students, When you come to a graduate school like this, you're 180 degrees away from where you started your education. When you first went to school, you sat at your desk, paid close attention and learned what the teachers were telling you. The teachers had been taught how to teach. Now you've come to the other extreme. You've come to a school where the faculty are outstanding, but they're like books in a library. You can get a tremendous amount of information out of books in a library, but you don't get it by sitting at a desk and hoping the books will teach you something. You've got to do the work of finding the book, taking it off the shelf and reading it. The faculty will teach the courses, but if you're really interested in the questions, don't wait for them to be intriguing teachers or to guess what you want. If you want to learn from them, you've got to do as you do with a book. Faculty members are willing to help you, but they're primarily interested in advancing their own discipline.

I'll mention one more innovation at the School of International Affairs. Columbia had the great advantage of working with the university's other outstanding graduate schools. SIA students who wanted a career in international law could take courses at the law school that fit the career they sought. If they wanted to go into business, they could take courses at the business school; and if they wanted to go into journalism, they could take courses at the journalism school.

But while many of our students went to work for the U.S. Government, Columbia had no school of public administration. I thought we should have a school of public administration, or at least a set of courses in the field, for people working for the government. I was told that that had been discussed before and decided against. So I asked the central administration about it and they said, No, we're not interested in that kind of thing.

I recruited experts from government to determine what we should be teaching and then brought in adjunct faculty to teach public administration. They were good enough that when I asked to be accredited as a school to teach public administration, we received the accreditation. So the School of International Affairs, SIA, changed to what it is now, the School of International Public Affairs and Administration, SIPA. Several years ago I gave SIPA the money to set up a mid-career education program for getting a master's degree in public administration. It is different from the program followed by younger students. It has a different set of courses, and it is administered differently and scheduled so a student can study and still hold a job. The program has been very successful.

One of the things I'd discovered when I was a student at Columbia was that when you were teaching a course, particularly with mid-career students, you had to be super-cautious, because you were apt to find a student or two who knew more about the subject than you did.

For example, one of the courses I took at Columbia included a look at the work of the National Science Board and the politics that surrounded it. I was most interested, of course, because I was on the National Science Board at the time. I knew more about the subject than the professor did, though I had the wits not to tell him. But it taught me not to assume that I knew as much about a subject as some students in my class.

There were very few conflicts with the faculty other than my wanting to introduce new courses. They'd been running things one way and I wanted to change that. I don't think the faculty was enthusiastic about the changes, but we got along just fine. It was the same thing with the university's central administration. They didn't always agree with me, but I thoroughly enjoyed our relationship.

I never went to a single graduation of mine—high school, college, graduate school, none of them. But as a dean at Columbia, I was condemned to twelve graduations. For every one of them I sat in hot academic robes in the damn rotunda and wished I were somewhere else.

Then it came time for handing out the diplomas to the graduating students. Since their families were willing to come, instead of standing on the rostrum and handing them out I went down to where each student and his or her family was sitting and gave them their diploma and told the family some good things about the student. That was a lot of work.

In 1983, when I got to retirement age, I decided to step out of the field, and my successor was appointed. Then I learned an important lesson. I went back to Columbia often. It was convenient, and I had many friends on the faculty. But I discovered that I was inadvertently undermining my successor, or at least so it appeared to me. I'd come in and the faculty would tell me what was wrong with my successor. I figured he didn't need somebody around who was making life more difficult for him. Although I disagreed with a lot of what he was doing, it was his show, not mine, so I stopped going to Columbia just to eliminate any problem that I might be causing.

I thoroughly enjoyed life as a dean. Being with this group of people was invigorating, and also a little exhausting. It was a wonderful period. As a matter of fact, looking back at my career, I never had a job I didn't like. I enjoyed being at sea in the Navy. I enjoyed being at the Rad Lab. I enjoyed Picker tremendously, and I enjoyed being a faculty member. I enjoyed serving on the National Science Board and doing the various jobs to which I was appointed by the federal government.

[20]

Philanthropy

I believe that philanthropy is a very, very serious pursuit that requires many of the same skills and attitude as running a business or a university. You have to really look into the subject and decide what you can do that would be beneficial. You don't do it on a basis of love: Joe is a friend of mine, and he wants some money for this. You do it because you've done the background research to be sure that you're doing something that will actually be the best use you can make of the money. You can give because you want to be considered a bountiful person, or you can give on the basis of—and this is true in my own experience—using the money to try to make things better. I feel that giving is a serious business investment, not a matter of whether you like the person or the project.

I'd remained deeply interested in education, and at Colgate I'd worn many hats: undergraduate, faculty member, member of the board of trustees and philanthropist. It was very much in my family's tradition to try to help projects we thought were good. When I graduated from Colgate, my family's graduation present to me was an endowed scholarship at Colgate. That was typical of my family. I was brought up to try to do things for others, and to believe that it's more important to be doing something constructive for them than to be doing other things.

One of the agreements Jean and I made early in our marriage was that any money I earned beyond what would be enough for the family to live on ought to be contributed to the public welfare one way or another, and that gifts ought to be made equally.

Jean had been a trustee of Smith, and Smith very much wanted Jean's papers for their archives. I tried to get Jean to agree, but for some reason she refused. She didn't want her papers archived. As it happened, some of them ended up there anyway, and I think it was a good thing, because they're damned interesting.

In any event, I think it was Jean who came up with the idea of helping to make it possible for students to intern in Washington, D.C., during the summer. We worked it out with the help of Thomas Corwin Mendenhall, the president of Smith, and our good friend Christine Beshar. It seemed very sensible to send people to Washington, where they could learn how to be good public servants. The program is called the Jean Picker Semester-in-Washington Program, and as you can imagine, it's very popular with students today.

Then we had another idea. This one was generated, I think, by Jean and me, not by the college. Smith was a leading institution with a need for really bright faculty members. Many faculty members, however, would rather go to a good research university than a good college. The question was how to get them to a college.

One answer was the Jean Picker Fellowships. Picker Fellows would be provided with funding for research while working on their doctorates and relieved of some of their teaching duties. All of them would convene each year to discuss their work with their colleagues, so that everyone learned something about everyone else's work. This helped the college compete with the research universities to recruit very high-quality faculty.

Later I suggested to Smith that I wanted to fund a major project now rather than after my death. Ruth Simmons suggested the engineering program. It seemed a very difficult thing to do. I'd seen the stress between academia and the professional fields. I assumed the same thing would happen at Smith, and I warned President Simmons. But we talked about it quite a bit, and I've got to hand it to Smith. The president found Dominic Delgrosso, who was the perfect person to head the new program. Due to his dynamism and charm and the fact that he knew exactly what he was doing, he won over the academic faculty and recruited large manufacturing companies like Ford to contribute to the program. It was a very bright idea, and very well carried out by Smith.

The first all-woman class of engineers graduated from the Picker Engineering Program in 2004. Jean would have been delighted.

The Picker family has endowed several things at Colgate. My parents endowed a scholarship as my graduation present. I endowed a fellowship for a professor of political science working in international affairs, and I endowed a professorship in the field of religion. This was more the university's choice than mine. I have to confess that being a Quaker, and not a very devout one, I am no expert on religion other than to believe firmly that it ought to be kept out of politics.

I gave Colgate its first computer classroom. I gave one of those to the School of International Affairs at Columbia too. These were the early days of computers and they are more common now, with students all having computers and showing what they're doing on a big screen at the front of the room.

I established the Picker Art Gallery at Colgate in 1969 in honor of my mother, who had made a gift to the college in 1964 so construction of an arts center could begin. I am no great aficionado of art—I am better at physics—but the gallery opened after my mother's death and was run quite well up until about eleven years ago, when its director retired. I think the dean of the faculty wanted to kill it off, because when I offered to provide funds for it, he said they didn't need the money, which is unusual for a college. A couple of years ago the gallery was practically dead. Then the new administration at Colgate hired Lizzie Barker as director. Lizzie had been working at the Metropolitan Museum of Art in New York. She did a wonderful job, and a recent gift to the art gallery was intended to encourage her. She made outstanding use of the gallery as a teaching tool, and to bring fine art to people in those areas of New York State where people don't get to art galleries very often.

I think, as I said to the provost of Colgate in 2007 when we launched the Harvey Picker Institute for Interdisciplinary Studies in the Sciences and Mathematics, that giving simultaneously money for a science institute and an improved art gallery represents, in my mind, the core mission of a college: to provide a broad spectrum so students will graduate with an understanding of the span of man's knowledge.

Several years ago I talked to a group of people from the nonprofit world, education and foundations, saying that it is important for a foundation to increase the efficiency of people it gives to, and not just give to good askers or people who perform well. I was shocked. I got a tirade in opposition. "We're not in business. We're running welfare," was their response.

I said, "On the other hand, if you were serving soup to five hundred people a day but could serve six hundred for the same cost because you operate more efficiently, wouldn't you like to do it?"

"Well, yes, but that's different."

I said, "No, that's what we're after. We're after doing the most you can do with the money you get."

So I think, and Jean did too, that giving is business. And serious donations require very serious thought as to exactly how and for how long this undertaking is going to operate.

I've always tried to convince people in the nonprofit arena to look for efficiencies. If a corporation wants to increase its output by fifty percent over the next ten years, it will try to figure out how to use the money it has to raise output by five percent annually. But a nonprofit will try to figure out how to raise five percent more money to increase its output.

Nor do I think that organizations should ever use money as an endowment. When I was at Columbia, I was very impressed at the number of endowed gifts there were for things like horse troughs, which was silly. If you give an organization $10,000 and tell them to stow it away in an endowment, that means a very large part of that $10,000 is going to be kept for the year 3000 or the year 5000. Let's see: It's only been 2,000 years since Christ lived. It would be kind of silly to get a gift back in Christ's age that you expect to be useful here and now. It's better that the institution spend the contribution at $1,000 a year. You could do that for 13 years because of the return on your investment. But give the project a finite life. If the organization could get $10,000 from you but can't raise it again in thirteen years, the organization probably doesn't deserve it.

I've had a whole range of experiences with nonprofits, going way back. The first nonprofit activity I ever participated in, something called Mobility Incorporated, in White Plains, New York, taught people who were handicapped how to become gainfully employed. I think Jean got me my place on the board. As a young man in my thirties, it was my first real introduction to being involved in nonprofit activities.

I served on the board of Mobility Incorporated, and on the boards of several hospitals, including New Rochelle, a suburban hospital, and Lenox Hill, in New York City. This little story gives a bit of insight into our current medical system.

I was the chairman of the board of New Rochelle Hospital when the head of the medical department, the chief of medicine, said he wanted to stop doing charitable work. When I demurred, he said, "Look at malpractice suits. There aren't any malpractice suits in our records brought by people who pay. The only such suits are those brought by the indigents we take care of. That's where all the malpractice suits are."

I said, "How does that happen?"

He said, "Well, some pregnant woman who is overweight and an alcoholic comes in for delivery. She hasn't seen anybody before, and she is in labor. They take care of her. She produces a defective child. We saved the child so she could keep it. Then the woman leaves the hospital. Some attorney will talk to her and say, 'How would you like an extra $50,000?' That sounds to her like a fortune. She says, 'Sure. How do I get it?' He says, 'I'll take care of that. I'll see that you get $50,000.'"

That's a very good insight into our malpractice system. If you look at it, it tends to be the university hospitals that get sued most often, and frequently a contest ensues between the doctor and the hospital. The doctor wants his reputation, so he wants to fight the case. The hospital wants to keep doing its work and not have to look at 10-year-old case records to write a report, so it settles, thereby undermining the doctor.

In the event of negligence or malpractice, hospitals and doctors should be penalized if they violate the rules. But the rule has to be there first, and it has to be sensible. There was a surgeon on our staff at New Rochelle Hospital who was clearly incompetent. He was somebody who should not have been a surgeon. So we faced the problem, and it was sad. I wanted to strip the surgeon of his hospital privileges, but the hospital's attorney said we couldn't do that because he would sue for loss of employment. The surgeon couldn't earn a living unless he was doing what he was doing.

What do you do in a case like that? Labor law says you have to keep an incompetent person, even one who is endangering patients. The only thing we could think of was putting the incompetent surgeon under supervision. He wasn't allowed to do anything in the operating room unless another surgeon was there to make sure he was doing it right. If he wasn't doing it right, they just got him out of there. That's a very expensive way of dealing with somebody who is incompetent. So we need to make rules, regulations and laws that are much tighter than they have ever been.

[21]
Politics

My politics are fairly left-leaning. Twice I was offered the task of Under-Secretary of Defense, once of Under-Secretary of State, and once—and this should make you laugh—of Chief of Protocol at the White House. While I would have liked to be able to accept any one of the three under-secretary jobs offered, I felt that I owed my first loyalty to my task at Picker X-Ray. As for the White House offer, I'd have been nothing short of a disaster as chief of protocol. The details of social niceties, precedence, etc., are not anything I want to know about or spend my days working on.

I did become heavily involved in the Johnson-Goldwater presidential race in 1964. Goldwater had advocated that the United States use nuclear weapons to win the Korean War. I was appalled at the idea, so I set out to do what I could to ensure that he was not elected. I helped organize a nationwide group called Scientists, Physicians and Engineers for Johnson. When he was elected, President Johnson felt that this organization had played a significant part in his victory. The reward was several invitations to Jean and me to White House dinners.

I was also asked to undertake several important jobs at the Department of State. The most interesting. I think, was being a delegate to the conference in Austria that laid the basis for the nuclear non-proliferation treaty. At that meeting, it took a tremendous amount of talking to small nations to get them to agree to a draft treaty to limit the spread of nuclear weapons. We had to persuade those nations not to build nuclear weapons and at the same time allow the big nations that already possessed the ability to produce nuclear weapons to go on making them. In return, we agreed to provide the small nations with all the knowledge they needed to be able to use nuclear energy to build their own devices, such as power stations, for non-weapon use. The United States worked hard to have that treaty ratified, and it was in effect until Pres. George W. Bush violated it in March 2006.

[22]

Wayfarer and Camden

I returned to the business arena in 1982 when I bought Wayfarer Marine Corp. in Camden, Maine. It was all Christine's fault. Let me go back a little. When Jean and I got married, I very much enjoyed sailing. Jean didn't know much about it, but as was typical of her, she decided that if I liked it, she'd try to help out. So I taught her how to sail, and she ended up being a better helmsman than I.

It was sheer joy to be with Jean, and one of the great pleasures of our married lives was to go off cruising together. We were both so busy in our careers that we had to plan a vacation at least a year ahead. We often made major decisions in our life while we were on these vacations, because we could get a perspective on the whole problem we were trying to solve instead of being influenced by recent, small events.

Jean and Harvey on Branta. *One of the great joys of their life was cruising on the ketch, which was designed for single- or double-handed sailing.*

Occasionally we'd invite other people along for our cruises, but it was usually just the two of us. We soon decided we wanted our own boat, and we knew exactly what we wanted. So we worked with Phil Rhodes, a very good naval architect, to design a craft for us. We designed not only the interior but the whole boat: where the rudder was to be in relation to the keel, what kind of propeller to add—in other words, we went through every aspect of how the boat was to look and handle. Built in Germany by Abeking and Rasmussen, it was one of the very first aluminum yachts in the world. We wanted to be able to take her out to sea, just the two of us, and Abeking and Rasmussen and Phil Rhodes did a magnificent job of making that possible.

Branta (this was the name of my father's boat; branta is Latin for the genus "goose," as *Branta canadiensus*, or Canadian goose) is a 45-foot ketch. The fact that I could sail that boat alone until just a few years ago is a tribute to her design. She was built at a time when all the electronics we have now to help you navigate weren't available. Jean and I used to cruise down east to Maine, at a time when people thought you were crazy to go up into those rocky shores with more heavy fog than anywhere else on the east coast of the United States. Now, with the advent of modern electronics, they are merely curious as to where to choose to spend the night and whether there is a good restaurant nearby.

The metamorphosis in the construction and navigation of small boats over the last half century has been phenomenal. Around the middle of the twentieth century, every small recreational boat (under seventy-five feet) was constructed of wood and navigated pretty much by good guessing, with the assistance of either good visibility or an occasional lighthouse or sound signal.

On days with poor visibility, you earnestly hoped that your guess as to the speed of the current out beyond the mouth of the river was accurate, but you had no way of ascertaining it. If you ended up stopping suddenly when you entered a harbor,

Gale, left, and Bobbi with their father on **Branta**. *Despite her evident terror, Gale became an avid and accomplished sailor. She also married one.*

unless it was a large one with a channel well marked by buoys, you'd found a ledge. Today few skippers know what "doubling the angle on the bow" is. Then it was a technique for finding out how far you were off the shore so you could pass that ledge safely.

Contrast that with today. The arcane, complex mysteries of coastal navigation have been replaced by the equivalent of a roadmap. Radar reveals any obstruction, be it floating or fixed, in your vicinity, as well as other craft headed in different directions and their proximity, and shows with absolute accuracy how far offshore you are. Your GPS shows you your position on an accurate map as well as water depth and any ledges or shoals in relation to your vessel. The result is that areas too difficult to navigate a few decades ago are now chock-full of small cruising boats, almost every one with a molded fiberglass hull. This new class of boat is less expensive to purchase and far less expensive to maintain.

Boating is no longer an activity limited to a few cognoscenti, each of whom belonged to an exclusive yacht club and practiced flag etiquette meticulously. The owners of the small motor and sailboats that fill the harbors and offshore waters no longer have to belong to a yacht club to obtain a mooring and probably don't know that there ever was such a thing as flag etiquette. All they now need is enough currency to pay a boatyard for fuel and a town for an overnight mooring.

Bringing *Branta* back to Larchmont from Maine one time, we had to get through a narrow passage with strong currents and a headwind. We needed the engine to get through. The engine wouldn't start, so I spent the next eight hours down in the engine room, getting the engine to work, while Jean navigated and sailed the boat. I got the engine to work and we brought the boat back home. I took it into the boatyard and said to the owner of the yard, "This is what went wrong, and this is what I had to do to fix it. I'd like you to do this and this so we don't ever have a repeat of this problem."

When I got through, the owner said, "You know, if you ever need a job as a mechanic, I'll hire you."

I thought about it for a moment—and this was just about when I was starting to think about retiring—and asked, "Would you really?"

He said, "Sure."

I said, "Okay, in two years I will retire from Columbia and I'll have time to work for you."

People thought that was ludicrous. But I had run a corporation, I had been in the Navy, I had done research, I had been a faculty member, I had been in education and I had had a lot of shots at doing things for the government. As a boat mechanic, I would have the chance to work with other sorts of people, people whose interests were different from my own, and to know for sure at the end of the day whether I'd solved the problem or not. And I couldn't take my work home with me. It looked like an ideal retirement job.

About a year or two after this, Christine Beshar called me and said, "Do you know Wayfarer Marine in Camden?"

I said, "Sure. You can't help knowing Wayfarer. It takes up about two-thirds of the inner harbor of Camden. But I've never used it. Why do you ask?"

She said, "Dick Watson and Tom Watson at IBM own Wayfarer, and as you know, Dick Watson has died, and Tom Watson, who is the ambassador to the Soviet Union, is thinking about selling it. Would you like to buy it?"

My reply was, "Christine, I may be a damn bad mechanic, but I don't have to buy a whole yard to get a job."

Out of curiosity, I came up and looked at the yard and found myself intrigued with the people. They were very much the old guild type: They did a good job because they wanted to maintain their reputation among their colleagues, not because the administration told them to do the job. I thought it would be an interesting thing to work with them, and I said to Charles "Mac" Macmullen, who was running the company, "Look, if you and the other people of the yard will stay, and if you will teach me about running a boatyard"—this was a repair yard, a place where you really worked on boats, not a marina—"then I'll think about buying it."

The next day, Mac told me he had talked to his colleagues and that everyone would be glad to have me buy the yard. Jean and I talked it over. We could spend time cruising the Maine coast. We'd keep *Branta* up there, and we wouldn't have a long slog up and back. I'd see what the yard was doing in the summer, and I'd go up once a month in the winter to act like an owner. But before I did anything, Tom decided not to sell the yard.

A couple of years later, Tom called me and said, "I understand you and I are going to the same conference on the Soviet Union that's being held in Hershey, Pennsylvania. Instead of you flying your plane and me flying my plane, why don't we both go in my plane?" That was an interesting suggestion, and we flew out in his plane. I learned more about Tom Watson than I'd ever thought I needed to know, but it was interesting, and just before the return flight ended, Tom turned to me and said, "You know, Harvey, Wayfarer is not up for sale, but I think you might do more with it than I would. If you want to buy it, I'll sell it to you."

So I called Christine and Tom called his attorney (they both worked for Cravath and had offices next to each other), and within a few weeks we got a letter that said, "If we do it one way, it's best for Tom. If we do it another way, it's best for Harvey. We think this is a good compromise."

Tom and I were meeting for lunch, because I wanted him to provide support for the Russian Institute at Columbia, which was one of the eleven research institutes that were under my tutelage. I didn't get any money for Columbia, but Tom did ask, "What did you decide about the yard?"

And I said, "Fine. I'll buy it."

And he said. "It's yours." That was the entire negotiation.

So I took over Wayfarer. Jean and I soon discovered that Camden was a lovely place. The interesting part for us was that the town had a very large community of people who were knowledgeable about and interested in international affairs. As I said often to Jean, Camden had all the advantages of a college town with none of the disadvantages of having students around. We'd expected to spend summers up there, but we discovered that the people in the town were so interesting that soon we decided we'd like to live there. Jean gave up her various posts in New York, as did I, and in 1982 we moved to Camden.

And that's how I got into the boatyard business.

As usual, I put in a lot of innovations. Wayfarer catered primarily to small sailboats and small motorboats. A small boatyard operation in the middle of a harbor is ridiculously stupid. You wouldn't put a carpentry shop on the most valuable land in a beautiful waterfront community like Camden. You wouldn't put a fiberglass shop or a paint shop there. You'd look for the least expensive land you could get. Yet this was what Wayfarer was doing, trying to make a living on a beautiful and very expensive piece of real estate. I decided that instead of working on and restoring a lot of small boats that the owners could work on themselves, Wayfarer should be a yard that was renowned for the great skill of its workers and able to work on large boats.

The normal thing in a boatyard is to haul a boat out and store it for the winter in an unheated, unventilated, unlighted shed. It's the cheapest thing you can do: Store boats, and then do repairs or renovation in a great rush in the spring when all the people want their boats. Of course, you could never do this, because more customers wanted their boat on June 1 than you could possibly accommodate. So I decided: "Let's do this like a real factory."

What do you do in a real factory? You get your incoming material and you put it in a storage facility where it's readily accessible. You take material from there and put it into a shop where you use it to produce what you're trying to produce. Then the finished product is returned to a storage facility until a customer buys it.

To do that, I rebuilt the sheds in the yard so you could get out any boat you wanted, at any time, without moving other boats. Previously, the sheds had been built so that you just stuffed things in from the entrance. You had to move the objects near the door out of the way in order to get the ones you wanted from the back.

We built a set of processing sheds—well-heated, well-lighted, well-ventilated—where you can do fine work no matter what the weather.

In the old days of the yard, boats were worked on where they were. What I proposed depended on the fact that nowadays you can pick up a large boat and move it readily to another location. That required expensive lifting and hauling equipment. But I was betting that over time this investment would reduce costs because repairs would take less time than working on the boats the old way.

As a result, during the first year I owned Wayfarer, for the first time, we delivered all but two yachts on time, and one was late because there was something wrong with the boat. Previously, nearly half the boats were delivered late.

To my puzzlement—and I have to admit that I hadn't really figured it out—it was also much less expensive to operate like this. The extra profit we made that first year was quite large. I divided the profits into thirds. One third went back to the customers as a rebate for the work we'd done for them; another third went to the workers; and the final third went into Wayfarer as capital.

Wayfarer prospered because it kept the workers busy for the whole long Maine winter. In the summer, our foolish customers wanted to use their boats instead of letting us continue to work on them!

The trend in the boating industry was toward larger boats. So I set out to get customers with larger, more sophisticated vessels that travel back and forth to the West Indies and cruise. We set up an organization in Antigua, the yachting center for the West Indies, to find a way to attract these boats to Maine. That meant prospective customers had to go past all the yards from Florida to Rhode Island, all the way up the coast, and come to Maine. It worked. Now, in the summer, you'll see lovely large yachts being worked on at Wayfarer.

Soon the yard had gained a reputation for having a highly skilled workforce and reasonable prices. It was also an attractive place for the crew to be during the summer. Owners of boats really don't care where the boat is for repairs, because they can have the crew bring it wherever they want. And Maine is a good place to cruise from, especially now that there are electronics for navigation and you are no longer bothered by the fog. You don't have to do any old-fashioned navigating. So Wayfarer did quite well.

I can tell you, though, that if you want to make money, it's dumb to go into the boatyard business. Nonetheless, I ran Wayfarer until 1997, when I decided to think about selling it, because I knew one of the unfortunate things I was going to have to do was die, sooner or later. I didn't expect to be around when I was ninety. I didn't want to leave that problem for somebody else to deal with. Besides, I didn't think I had any more bright ideas about the boatyard. I felt as though I'd done my share.

I felt very strongly that Camden ought to have a working waterfront and not be like many town harbors in Maine that are now lined with condominiums. One of Camden's main sources of income was tourists, and yacht owners are the best kind of tourist to have. Indeed, I'd spoken to the owners of several stores in town, and they all said: "We make more money from the yachts you have in the yard than we do from the busloads of people that come to visit Camden."

I thought that for the good of Camden, we want to keep the yard going. Otherwise the land would be sold for its "highest and best use": condominiums. Finally I found two people, Parker Laite Sr. and Jack Sanford, who live in Camden and who were competent and willing to buy the yard. The basis of the sale was, as I used to tell people who were interested in buying it, "Let me tell you that just because you meet my price doesn't mean you get the yard. As far as I'm concerned, this is an application for a job. If you meet my price and convince me that you'll keep the yard going for the next few years in very much the way it works now, so that the big yachts will keep coming, you can have the boatyard. But you've got to be dedicated to keeping Wayfarer operating."

Naturally, that limited the number of people I could sell it to. But Parker and Jack did a marvelous job of keeping the yard going, and resisting the temptation to line the harbor with condominiums.

Boatyards are different from other factories. There is something there for the visitor to see. You can stroll through it—in some ways it's kind of crazy to let the public into your working place—but I think it adds to Camden's attractiveness.

[23]
Life in Maine

Living in Maine, I developed a great interest in the area of public policy. I served on the Maine Healthcare Finance Commission (MHCFC), beginning in about 1989, and then in 1992 on the Maine Commission to Overhaul the Workers' Compensation Insurance System.

At the time, hospitals were under the state's jurisdiction. The objective of the Maine Healthcare Finance Commission was to see that the system ran efficiently. There were several interesting aspects to that. Hospitals had to get the commission's permission to make innovations, and they had to report to us their financial status on a regular basis. We were charged with minimizing costs and at the same time ensuring that a well-run healthcare system was in place. This included making sure that hospitals did not overcharge but did survive. We saw to it that hospitals received regular monthly payments so that they didn't go through peaks and valleys of cash flow.

At the same time, the mission was to make sure that hospital charges were consistent; that patients were not overcharged; and that the hospitals did not spend an inordinate amount of money on new technology and other equipment or buildings. Yet another objective was to make sure that funds were allocated properly to each hospital, and that the hospitals, knowing what their income would be, could continue budgeting to ensure that they would not operate at a loss if they followed directions.

One of the problems I did help solve during my four years on the commission was the question of how to decide how much each hospital could spend on new technology. From a statewide point of view, we didn't want two hospitals in the same town to acquire expensive MRI equipment instead of sharing one, especially if the money could be used somewhere else to greater advantage. I came up with a formula for developing such hospital budgets. My friends on the commission decided to call it the Picker formula. It was really a simple mathematical solution that allowed us to stop arguing about the details of who should get what, and to settle on the total budget and a plan for how the monies should be allocated.

The hospitals chafed under the restrictions we placed on them and fought very hard to get rid of the commission. They succeeded when the HMOs came in. Jock McKernan was governor at the time. When I went to talk to him about the situation, he said, "Harvey, I suppose you're here to tell me that the healthcare commission ought to be retained."

I said, "Not at all. I think the HMOs will be very effective at keeping hospital income down. And as long as there's such a strong feeling that it's a better way to go, that's the thing to do. But that isn't going to make it any cheaper for patients. HMOs expect to make a profit, or they wouldn't be there, and the cost of the administrative apparatus to keep them going is going to increase the cost of healthcare to the patient, with the smaller part of the dollar going to the actual cost of clinical care. I'd suggest that you look into something that is important: What proportion of the healthcare dollar will actually be spent on clinical care, and how much will be dispensed in overhead and accounting? And you ought to get a record of that right now to compare what will change when the HMOs come in."

The governor didn't think very much of that idea, but he finally agreed to set up a panel to look into it. Unfortunately, that panel was largely made up of representatives of the hospital association and the HMOs. They created a survey, and despite my urging against it, they—and this was no surprise at all—produced a set of statistics that didn't mean a damn thing and would be ignored, as it should have been.

A couple of years later, one night in 1992, I was sitting at home in front of my computer when the telephone rang. The caller said, "Hello, Harvey, this is Jock." I didn't remember knowing anybody named Jock, but for once in my life I had the sense to keep quiet. I soon realized it was the governor calling—no secretary, no nothing, just like your friend calling you from around the corner—and he said, "As you probably know, Maine's in deep trouble with its workers' compensation system. We're appointing a small blue-ribbon commission, only three or four people, to see if we can get this thing straightened out."

I said, "Governor, you don't want me. I don't know any more about workers' compensation than what the two words mean when you put them together."

He said, "Fine. That qualifies you."

Well, I found out that what had happened was that the workers' comp system in Maine was deeply in debt, flat broke. It was so expensive that many large companies were leaving

Maine because the cost of workers' comp had gone sky-high. Up until five years earlier, about 120 companies were selling workers' comp insurance. Now there were five, and four of them had said they were going to leave by the end of the year.

This commission was given the task of trying to solve that problem. The legislature had tried for five years with no success whatsoever—in fact, the situation had continued to deteriorate. We were given about four months to come up with a report.

None of us knew anything about workers' comp insurance, so we attended public hearings to give ourselves a crash course in why it was a problem and where and how it was being done better. I discovered, among other things, that sunshine laws sharply restrict what you can do to be innovative. In a private meeting you can say, "Hey, guys, this seems like a crazy idea, but should we consider it?" You don't do that when you are going to be quoted in the newspapers the next day. You limit yourself to saying things that will reassure everyone that the members of the Blue-Ribbon Commission are not crazy.

We came up with a report in about three months. It was submitted to the legislature, and the legislature started to modify it. Governor McKernan said, "No, you can't modify it."

And the legislature said, "But, governor, we're supposed to do our job, and this is required by our job."

The governor said, "Okay. You can offer suggestions, and if the Blue-Ribbon Commission accepts them, I'll agree to them. If the Blue-Ribbon Commission doesn't accept them, I'll veto the law."

Remember that there was a lot of pressure on everyone, because if our report wasn't accepted there would be no system. There was a huge storm of protest against the report, including very heavy lobbying efforts, because we had eliminated the use of the courts for settling workers' comp cases. We said that unless it was a constitutional question, there would be no trials in court, and that claims would be settled by a commission set up to do just that.

It turned out that some attorneys were getting two-thirds of any settlement and making millions of dollars a year. Of course, they didn't like the idea of losing all that income, and they paraded injured people limping up and down the legislature's steps and all the rest of it. But I have to say for Governor McKernan that he remained adamant. He didn't intend to let our work go for nothing.

The legislature submitted a group of amendments to us. We looked at some of them and said, "That's fine. Let's use it." Others we looked at and said, "No way—that will wreck the system. Can you redo it?" Of the third group we said, "Yes. We'll do this if you'll modify it a little bit to say something else." Really, we had the first and last word on it.

At the same time as we changed the workers' comp system, we looked at the possibility that no insurance company would be willing to take on the task in the future. The state was down to only one company. We didn't want to create a state-run insurance company, because if we did and it was unsuccessful, it would cost the taxpayers money. And if it was successful, the state would borrow all the money from it. Neither alternative seemed to be good. So we set up an insurance company, mainly with smoke and mirrors (and I think we could have taught Enron a thing or two about how we did this).

After a long fight, the legislature approved the plan the way we wanted it. The president of the insurance company we created would serve on the workers' comp board, and we searched for that person. We found an ideal man. My colleagues on the search committee said he was too expensive. I said, "Nobody who can run this company well can be too expensive."

Within three years of the new law going into effect, the cost of workers' comp in Maine dropped fifty percent. Despite the fact that payments to individuals were increased, the insurance company was very profitable, and the number of accidents dropped by fifty percent.

How did we succeed? How did we cut costs so rapidly? We started on the basis that we were not going to fight, as insurance companies do, about whether a worker is covered and if the compensation should be that high. We worked on the basis that if the board in charge of this says this is what the worker ought to get, that's what he will get, and we're not going to argue about it. An injured worker is entitled to what he ought to get, and we won't use an attorney unless the other side uses an attorney.

So we cut out those costs, but, more important, we said, "Our job is not to pay these people more or less; our job is to prevent accidents."

Here's how we cut the accident rate: We said that if the CEO of the company wants insurance from us, we will ask him to spend a day with us being trained in what he has to do and what our values are, and we'll give his company a ten percent discount for his attendance. This program of going into organizations and training them how to prevent accidents resulted in fewer accidents.

When you run an insurance company, the rate you charge your client's organization is based on history. If the organization subsequently suffers fewer accidents, that's very profitable for the insurance company, which bases fees on the prior accident rate rather than on accidents that occur currently. So the insurance company benefits. The workers benefit by being exposed to fewer hazards. And the organization benefits, because the next year its premium drops because it has a better record, and that continues from year to year. As we reduce the accident rate, the insurance company gets more profitable and the insured company pays lower premiums. The system works very well.

This experience taught me something very important: You should never, ever use the legislature to create a system. The legislature, just by the way it's set up, is incapable of creating an efficient system. Why? Because each member of the legislature wants some detail to be optimized to please her or his constituents. It sounds good, but none of them is trained to look at how you can get the whole organization to work. You need something like our commission to do it.

I was interested in issues at the local as well as the state level, and I served on the personnel committee for the town of Camden. What the employees of this small town government were paid, and how much extra they were paid, was determined by the town's select board. It was sometimes true that if members of the board liked you, you were paid more. And if they didn't like you, you didn't advance.

When I became chairman of the personnel committee, we worked out a system that's been used ever since. It determines payments based on what people in similar positions in this area of Maine are paid. Upgrades in pay and rank are automatic. The system is still in use today.

I worked on many other things. I served on the local board and became chairman of Kno-Wal-Lin, the area's home healthcare agency. Kno-Wal-Lin provides nursing and other services for home care.

I was also on the board of the Midcoast Mental Health Association, which gave me an insight into what is done to care for people who are mentally ill. It was a shock to discover how bad mental healthcare is in the United States. The single most egregious culprit is the idea of confidentiality. Confidentiality shields every psychologist, social worker, psychiatrist and anybody else against any kind of quality control. Without quality control, mental healthcare in this country is probably no better today than it was on the day the Pilgrims landed.

The people who suffer from mental illness must wait inordinate lengths of time even to be diagnosed. The only time judgment is swift is in an acute case where someone is openly showing signs that he wants to commit suicide or murder somebody. Even then the judgment is sometimes made by someone who may or may not have the qualifications to make it.

I strongly believe that the whole idea of confidentiality in mental healthcare has to be eliminated and the consequences faced. It's exactly analogous to those days in medicine when you didn't talk about venereal diseases, so nothing was done to cure them or the cures were terrible. There was a moral dimension, a feeling that somebody who has a venereal disease had done something wrong, so we shouldn't even bother to research how to cure it. Mental health is in a similar state, where we can't let it be known that patient A or patient B has a mental health problem, even though it may be glaringly obvious. The whole system still works on the premise that mental illness is such a shameful thing that we can't talk about it.

You can't know how the quality of care is compromised when certain individuals may or may not be competent to make judgments. The state has a set of standards, and it checks rigorously to see how closely you're meeting the standards. But the state checks by seeing whether every card has the right initials on it. It's a complete paper inspection. It has nothing to do with the actual patients or the way they're being cared for. There is no incentive to do better or to do research, except to produce a paper trail. It's an absolute farce. The state refuses to renew your license if certain people haven't signed off on the card, but it doesn't give a darn about what happens to the patient.

I have serious reservations about a country that has by far the most powerful military force in the world, is stronger than all the rest of the countries put together and spends money on new, more complicated and more foolish devices to the huge benefit of corporations—but that can't afford to provide healthcare, education or better housing to the indigent. I'd suggest that those who claim they're being guided by God look a little bit at what Jesus had to say.

Camden Public Library

Soon after Jean and I moved to Camden, she was asked to serve on the board of the local library. She served for quite a while, until she became too ill. She died in 1990, and a year later the chairman of the board of trustees asked me to come to the library. There, in a prominent place in front of the library, the Jean Picker Garden had been planted. A plaque in the entrance explained how each of the flowers in the garden was related to Jean. I was very moved by this tribute. And when they asked me to replace her on the board, I agreed.

After I'd been on the board a couple of years, I was elected chairman. I told my colleagues that I thought they were making a great mistake and would rue the day. I believed that the library, a beautiful building in a magnificent setting, next to an amphitheater (designed by a very prominent historical architect and, as his only public work, of real historical importance), was old-fashioned and too small for the town. The librarian scowled if you took out a book because she wanted it in the library, not in your hands, and she wouldn't allow a child to talk in the library because libraries were places for silence.

At Columbia, I had had considerable experience with what was probably one of the world's largest and finest collections of books on international affairs, and I knew something about how to run research libraries. I didn't know a thing about community libraries. But I looked at it and said, "This is too small. We've got to build a larger library while keeping the library we've got here."

That raised the question of how to do that. The library itself was a historic building, and so were the grounds. How do you make a bigger library when you can't change the building and you can't change the grounds? There were lots of ideas about building a second library nearby, or somewhere else.

At the School of International Affairs, we had a huge library, but it was—like many other extensive libraries—largely underground. It occupied three very large areas, one over the other. I suggested that we build a new library under the old library and not interfere with the grounds.

I also suggested that we get the library built within a year, though there were no plans yet and no idea of how to build it, and that we raise all the money we need in nine months so we'd have the money before construction was complete.

The construction of an underground library turned out to be a very challenging undertaking. We had a superb local architect who came in every morning to make sure that every bit of stone or brick or any other work was perfect. But we soon ran into a problem. We had thought that the old library, like most such buildings, was supported by footings under its outer walls. It turned out that it was supported under its outer walls not only by footings but also by support piles, and that piles supported the library as well. We had to dig under the building to put in the basement. But how did you dig under a library to get at those support piles without risking collapse? We finally discovered that the equipment used to dig mines could get around those support piles and reinforce them.

The day before the opening of the library, my daughter Gale and I, along with the other invited guests, were taken through the library to see it ahead of the public. We were pleased at how well this very new design had turned out. A board member said to me, "Did you see the audiovisual room?"

And I said, "Yes. It looks like it will be very nice."

He said, "Did you look above the door?" And my daughter and I looked above the door and saw that it was called the Jean

Picker Room. This had been done without my knowledge, and it was a delight.

The next day was the dedication. It had been very carefully planned. Among the speakers was former First Lady Barbara Bush, whom I knew quite well. I sat next to her at the ceremony. Toward the end of the ceremony, one of the trustees got up to speak, and to my intense irritation, he started to speak about me. I said to Barbara, "This has no place in the dedication of the library. We've got to stop him."

Barbara just looked at me. It turned out that the new library had been dedicated to me, and when I went in, I saw a large plaque. I'd been in the library the night before and it hadn't been there then. Apparently it had been put up during the ceremony so I wouldn't know about it. I would have stopped it if I could have.

We all had a great time making this wonderful library happen. Not only did we build an underground library, but it was the first community library in Maine to have computers. I'd asked someone from the New York Public Library to talk to us about the role of computers in libraries and the problems of installing them there, and eventually we built a whole computer section.

My theory in those early days was that you don't have to teach children about computers. They're all going to learn how to use them anyhow. It's their parents who aren't going to learn. And it's their parents who need to know, because computers are the future. So we put in a flock of computers. We also put in a room where small children could play and get to know and like the library. And we put in a conference room large enough for people to come for lectures and with the audiovisual technology needed for that. These were quite remarkable changes.

I was greatly pleased to have been part of so much of what was new in the library. A few days after the dedication, I walked into the library and a parent was going out with a crying three-year-old on his shoulder. And I said, "I bet you're taking her away from the computer in the children's room."

And he said, "Yes. How did you know?"

Eventually we were able to help educate other Maine community libraries in how to budget for, buy and install computers. So our innovation turned out well for the whole state.

Mid-Coast Forum on Foreign Relations

Jean and I were both very interested in foreign affairs. I had done a lot of traveling overseas for Picker X-Ray, which had dealerships in almost every non-communist country of any size, and Jean's service as a U.S. delegate to the UN had given her considerable international experience.

When we moved to Maine, Jean and I found that a great many people who had worked for the State Department or the CIA or another government organization had retired to Camden, and were very interested in and knowledgeable about international affairs. That, in fact, was one of the things that led us to settle in Camden.

But before we'd settled there, a group, including Jean, had gotten together to meet regularly and discuss international affairs. It was decided to limit the group to fifty people, and Jean and I were asked to join. "But we don't live here," we said. So the group very kindly held two places open for when we did finally move to Camden.

We were quite active in the organization, called the Mid-Coast Forum on Foreign Relations. It's been very successful, and it still has a waiting list with more people on it than there are members in the group. It meets once a month with a visitor who is distinguished in one aspect or other of international affairs. It makes the community much more interesting. And it's become so popular that the real problem is that lots of people want to join because it's an awfully good group to have lunch with.

The Camden Conference

For some time I'd contemplated Camden, with all its bed-and-breakfasts and hotels and restaurants, as a wonderful place to hold something like the Aspen Institute, in the wintertime, when the town was fairly empty. In 1987, our friend Bob Tierney suggested that we have a conference in Camden on international affairs with outstanding speakers.

That first Camden Conference went on to become an annual event, presenting outstanding speakers on complex subjects and drawing hundreds of people from around Maine and the rest of the country.

From the start we had no problem getting speakers, because all the members of the committee knew people of importance in government and in academia. The conference has continued to grow and prosper, and it is now an important event in Maine. Its coverage of such topics as the Middle East, the worldwide energy crisis and the economic impact of China on the world was just the kind of thing we'd love to have at a good university for a three-day seminar.

One of the basic truths of life is that when you're young, you don't get the credit you deserve, and when you're old, you get much more credit than you ever deserved. I've been reaping a lot of that all the way along. I've gotten a Townsperson of the Year award and an award from the Rotary Club for the things I've done, although I've never been a member of the organization. I've gotten a lot of very nice tributes and articles about me in various publications.

About a dozen years ago, to my great surprise, I got an award from the National Electrical Manufacturers Association of the United States for outstanding leadership in the field of X-rays. That goes back to my days in the X-ray industry. I also received awards from radiological societies as well as honorary memberships.

I've also been awarded a number of honorary degrees—Colgate, Smith, the University of New England. At Smith, I stood up and said, "I may be one of the few people who ended up a Smith graduate while being male."

The University of New England graduation, in 1997, was an interesting occasion. I was invited to accept an honorary degree and found that the other person receiving one was named George Bush. When he and I were seated on the stage, I realized that it was the George Bush I knew, George Bush the elder.

I listened to him talk and was absolutely flabbergasted when he said to the audience, "Do you remember my 'thousand points of light' talk? Well, I'm proud today to be on the same rostrum with one of the shining points of light of the United States, Harvey Picker."

[24]
The James Picker Foundation

Picker X-Ray was very successful after World War II. In 1947, a couple of years after I had returned to the company, my father and I decided to set up a foundation in his honor. It seemed appropriate that it should have something to do with healthcare as well as X-rays.

I was assigned to figure out how to set up the James Picker Foundation and how to run it. Most fortunately for me, Dr. Alan Gregg, then the head of the Rockefeller Foundation, generously found time to provide guidance and answer questions in regard to organizational structure. What he said has always stuck in my mind: "Running a foundation is quite a bit like investing in the stock market. If everything you do turns out to be successful, you're being too conservative. If nothing you do succeeds, you're being too radical. You need a good mixture of both in your portfolio."

It had not been decided what the foundation's objective was to be or how it was to be governed. Luckily, four of the leading academic radiologists in the country gave us superb advice on those issues. They pointed out that radiology was not highly regarded as a medical specialty—it was still considered to be similar to photography, and radiologists nothing more than photographers—and therefore it did not attract the brightest, most innovative medical students. Indeed, many medical schools didn't even have a course in how to read X-rays.

The purpose of focusing on academic radiology was to highlight its benefits to people through both diagnosis and treatment. Academic radiologists were specially trained to do research and to diagnose difficult cases. If the best and brightest could be attracted to the specialty, it would be through academic radiology.

On the advice of our advisors, we set out to attract the highest-qualified graduating physicians to the field of academic radiology.

Every member of the board of trustees of the James Picker Foundation was a highly respected radiologist. They were so dedicated to their work that there was no need for a staff, so all the assets were used for fellowships or project grants, which were administered by the board members themselves. The grants were available to bright young people, or even mid-career radiologists, who could become eminent teachers and improve the science.

Unlike today, when radiology is highly paid, radiologists at that time were paid very little. The James Picker Foundation did much to improve that situation. It gave grants for many purposes, from helping radiologists learn business administration because they were running large, expensive departments, to enabling young radiologists to go to Sweden, which was far ahead of us in the field, to do research and study the most advanced techniques at the time.

The foundation helped attract and educate some very important radiologists. As a group, the Picker Fellows, being bright and effective, really made a difference in various aspects of radiology. The field started to attract more good people, and the recipient of a Picker Foundation grant or fellowship was regarded very highly. In fact, Picker Fellows were so successful that the Radiological Society of North America, which is by far the largest and most prestigious radiological organization in the world, gave an award to my father, which he very much deserved. Much later, I was made an honorary member of RSNA, even though I'm no radiologist, and only radiologists or those in related specialties such as physicists were eligible to become members. And even later, both Jean and I were awarded gold medals by the Association of University Radiologists.

The Picker Fellows program was so prestigious that when the federal government at last stepped in and started giving similar but larger grants, promising young radiologists who were offered both would pick a Picker Fellowship because it would do more for their career than taking a larger scholarship from the government. Eventually it became clear that the foundation had accomplished its objective, and radiology was such a highly paid profession that we no longer needed to recruit good people into it. By that time my father was no longer involved with the foundation, and Jean and I decided there wasn't much point in continuing in that field.

In 1986, the James Picker Foundation had $15 million in assets. Jean and I looked around for another field that a small foundation could have an impact on. We finally hit on something that was to become the genesis of "patient-centered care."

[25]

The American Way of Dying

The desire in medicine is to keep people alive no matter what. The way my mother and my sister died was so terrible that it left me with a great fear that American medicine cannot see the difference between death and dying. I am reminded of My Lai, in Vietnam, where the innocent people of the village were killed because, the generals said, they wanted to save the village.

My mother died after prolonged suffering. Her suffering was the result of a medical decision that caused a very long, painful and unnecessarily unpleasant period of her life. Then my sister died of pancreatic cancer, but not before she went through a prolonged period of terrible pain that medicine couldn't ameliorate. The physicians caused this terrible period by keeping her alive.

I feel very strongly about this. Torquemada, the Spanish monk who became the first Grand Inquisitor of the Spanish Inquisition, tortured people to save their souls. But the torture lasted at most no more than three days. American medicine has learned how to torture patients for months—or more, if necessary. This is an improvement I think we can live without. In fact, this appears to be the triumph of the medical fraternity over God's will.

My mother was an invalid, and partly paralyzed. She had a disease characterized by an inadequate flow of blood to the extremities. As a result, she developed ulcers on her feet and was admitted to Columbia-Presbyterian Hospital in New York. The doctors there tried to alleviate the problem but couldn't. They said the only solution was to amputate her leg.

Now my mother had, before going to the hospital, pleaded with me not to let her become a complete invalid. She said she would much rather die. The doctors listened to my request not to amputate the leg but then came to me and said, "Gangrene has set in, and if you let your mother die this way it will be a horrible death. The only thing to do is to amputate the leg."

I certainly didn't want to see my mother tortured. I figured that amputation, as bad as it was, was the only solution, and the leg was amputated. I kept insisting that this woman wants to die and has a right to. Fortunately for me, and for my mother, she developed pneumonia. It probably would have killed her. I spent long hours trying to get the doctors not to treat the pneumonia but let it run its course. I knew she'd probably die in a week or two, but I knew that was what she wanted, and she had a right to what she wanted. It was a terrible, terrible struggle with the doctors, but I finally got their agreement.

I visited the hospital early every morning to see my mother, and I walked in one day and saw that she was getting fluids intravenously.

On inquiry, I discovered she was being given antibiotics. I got hold of the doctors and said, "How did this happen? We agreed that this would not happen."

They said, "Well, some intern walked in during the night and figured she had pneumonia and started the IV."

You didn't have to be an intern to diagnose that my mother had pneumonia. You could have diagnosed it without getting near her.

And I said, "Well, stop it," and the doctors and nurses said, "That's impossible. under the current conditions. If we stop it, we get into a tremendous amount of trouble. Nothing will make us. There's no way to stop it and nothing can be done to stop it."

My mother survived. She hated every minute of the years that she lived as an invalid, lying in bed, a prisoner in an institution. This bright, intelligent, accomplished woman would have done better in a jail; she wouldn't have been so isolated. For somebody who led a highly productive life, this was a hell of a way to deal with it.

My sister was a physician. She had studied medicine at a time when there were very few women in the field. She was a first-rate pediatrician, very well liked by parents as well as children and really an asset to the community. Her youngest child developed brain cancer and was treated by radiation. The child was afraid to stay in the room alone, so my sister and I took turns being in the room when the radiation treatment was given. I got the reluctant agreement of my sister to stay behind a very heavy lead shield that the hospital provided for us so we would get minimal radiation.

I didn't find out until long afterward that when her son became too upset, my sister came out from behind the lead shield to hold him while he was being treated. She developed cancer of the pancreas, which is very, very painful. My sister was a heavy smoker, and I know that smoking contributes to cancer. She took care of her two surviving children for a while. But as the cancer began to take its toll, she became bedridden, and the pain became so great that it couldn't be controlled with any pain medication that the doctors would prescribe.

At that point, it was clear that this woman was being tortured unmercifully. The right thing to do was to stop life support; otherwise, we were condemning her to worse pain than you could have produced in a torture chamber. Life support kept her alive and in pain for weeks unnecessarily, not to speak of the expense of the care.

I came away from these experiences with a strong feeling that medics enjoy playing God instead of leaving it to God. It's very, very cruel. I'm not suggesting that you kill people who are dying, but I am suggesting that people be allowed to control what they want to do.

In Maine, where I live, we have a very strict advanced-directive law that emphasizes all along, in something like four or five pages, the patients' right to make their own decision. But the last paragraph says that if the doctors of the hospital don't follow the advanced directive, there is no penalty. I think it is pretty much a political, religious and social problem, and very much a comment on the American healthcare system.

It might seem that the genesis for our interest in patient-centered care was Jean's negative experience with the healthcare system. But in fact it was quite the reverse. Jean spent a lot of time in hospitals due to her ailment, and I'd see a young doctor, a resident, come in and ask her the standard things before she went to sleep. For better or worse, the doctor usually had only three minutes to spend with her because he had to get on with his work. But I'd come back twenty minutes later and he'd still be sitting next to Jean, chatting away.

Jean had a way of engaging doctors' interest, and it would be great if every patient was able to do what Jean did. But the problem really was what we saw happening to other people.

You don't have to go far to see doctors treat people terribly—they come in reading about the patient's case, since they haven't even taken the time to do that, and then they start to leave. Obviously Jean and I spent a lot of time in hospitals, and it was this intense exposure that made it possible for me to see what went on.

But it wasn't a secret. You could see the same thing in any hospital. A trustee of Columbia Presbyterian Hospital once said to me, "Every patient gets very good service, and we're doing a wonderful job." When I asked whether he'd walked through the waiting rooms, he said, Yes, he had, and he never saw anybody. I wondered whether his vision should be tested. I mean, you'd have to be pretty damn impervious to humans not to see them. But he was sold on his job as a trustee.

[26]

The Picker Surveys

Jean and I recognized that by the middle of the twentieth century, medical care had swung from one end of the pendulum to the other. Up to then, there wasn't much a doctor could do to help a patient get over pneumonia or any other really serious illness. He had a limited number of effective medicines, so the most he could do was to assure good nursing care and his comforting presence.

With the advent of antibiotics and the development of vastly improved diagnostic equipment, doctors no longer make house calls, since you can't diagnose an illness or treat a patient at home as well as you can in an office. This was a sharp contrast to the first half of the twentieth century, when you could diagnose most illnesses as easily out of your medical kit as in a hospital.

Medical care moved from being largely humane—trying to build up the patient so the patient could withstand the disease—to the opposite pole: "We don't care who the patient is. If this is the disease, this is how you treat it." And so a patient went from being Mrs. Jones in Room 203, who has a stomach problem, to the ulcer problem in 203, whose name is, I think, Mrs. Jones.

Accordingly, the new objective of the James Picker Foundation was to direct medical treatment back to being concerned with patients as human beings, not just the subjects of clinical studies, and to treat them once again as human beings with worries and concerns and meet their nonclinical needs too.

In the early twentieth century, nurses were someone you knew, someone who cared for you. Now a nurse is the voice over the intercom asking, "What do you want?" You don't know the nurse's name and she doesn't care who you are, only that it's time to give you an injection or take your temperature.

So we set out to reemphasize the need for basic care. It was obvious that the radiologists on the board of the foundation, most of whom were quite old, weren't going to be the right people for this endeavor. Much to my dismay, they also didn't remember to stay alive. They kept dying off.

In 1986, one of the members of the board was Margaret Mahoney, who was the president of The Commonwealth Fund. Jean and I knew Maggie well. We thought she had a better view of the nonprofit world than anybody else we knew. Jean, Maggie and I agreed on the importance of supporting research into the aspect of medical care that was concerned with treating patients as though they were human beings instead of bodies with a disease. Since Jean and I were also getting on in years, we decided the best way to continue this project was to turn it over to an excellent foundation to carry on the work. We had great confidence in the people at The Commonwealth Fund, so we asked them to take all the assets of the James Picker Foundation with the understanding that they would develop the Picker program based on patient-centered care.

Under Maggie, Commonwealth ran this program very well. A superb organization, it was, and is today, the leader in the field, and there's still a small Picker program there dedicated to improving the lot of frail elderly people.

Sometime during the 1980s, I discovered that the research generated by the Picker programs was excellent but that it wasn't having a hell of a lot of impact. Results were being published in very reputable scientific journals, but they weren't affecting the actual practice of medicine.

When you don't know which way is going to lead you into the light, you go down a lot of blind alleys. At first we spent quite a bit of money learning what not to do and what wouldn't achieve our purpose. We also spent a lot of time thinking and talking about how we could make this program of focusing more attention on patient care more effective.

While this was going on, Maggie Mahoney and the people at The Commonwealth Fund came up with a startlingly obvious idea that we all should have thought of in the first place: If you want to see that patients' emotional and physical needs are met, how about asking patients what's important to them and how they feel they are being treated?

The end result, the Picker Surveys, were by no means the first in the field. Hospitals have sent out questionnaires for years to find out how patients reacted. These questionnaires, however, ask the president of the hospital or the chairman of the medical committee or somebody like that to give the answers.

We created a fund to underwrite research at Harvard University to develop a really scientifically accurate questionnaire to determine the answers to questions about patients' needs.

To get answers that were useful, you had to do two different things. First and foremost, it occurred to the Harvard-Picker team that the way to find out what is important from a patient's point of view is, surprisingly, to ask the patient. So they gathered group after group of patients after they had been discharged from the hospitals where they had been treated and asked them, "What was important to you? What did you care about? What pleased you? What worried you? What could the hospital have done to make you feel better?"

That seems pretty obvious, but at the time that was not what was done. After the researchers found out what was important, the questions were reviewed to make sure that they'd been asked in a way that would elicit statistically relevant answers. If you asked "You didn't care about the quality of the food, did you?" you got a different answer from "What did you feel about the quality of the food?" They collected a large group of questions from these discussion groups, issues that not only affected the patient but that could be addressed in a meaningful way.

One of the questions on the questionnaire was "Do you think you would have suffered less pain if more attention had been paid to you?" If a hospital asked that question and eight percent of the patients said, "Yes, I think if more attention had been paid to me, I could have suffered less pain," that didn't tell the hospital too much. Was the eight percent the inevitable result, or did other hospitals do better? Were some hospitals doing remarkably better?

You had to ask the question not as true or false but as how does something compare with the best that can be done by hospitals. This is the origin of the use of the term "best practices" as the standard. Going back to the question about pain, if eight percent of your patients tell you about pain as the result of not getting enough attention, and the average per hospital in your area is twelve percent , you can pat yourself on the back and say, "I'm doing quite well."

While these questions don't have standard answers, they're questions that you can answer uniformly with, Can others do better? If they do better, then we can learn from them. If, on the other hand, they are doing worse, they can learn from us. You're looking at what the patient experienced, but you're also measuring what the expectation is. So when you make comparisons across countries, as we are able to do by having a standard questionnaire, it may or may not be clear that you're actually being treated better in country A than in country B, or that your expectations are lower in country A than in country B. Within your own country, however, you're sure of getting some answers. So when we hold our training seminars, we don't tell people how to solve a problem. We bring in people who have shown that they can consistently do better on the issue than others, and we ask them to explain how they do it. That is the way you improve: You're always trying to do as well as those who do best.

In order to develop a national survey to find out what was the norm, the Harvard-Picker team set out to survey comparable institutions across the nation. We wondered how university hospitals compared to each other. We wondered how city hospitals compared to each other, and how small rural hospitals compared to each other. The results would indicate what kind of care you could expect in various places.

We also wanted to know what was normal for the region. People in New England may expect things that are different from what people in Texas expect, so we wanted to get a flavor of what the people in various regions expect. We decided it would take sixty hospitals to give us adequate classifications. We were surprised, when we did it, at how many hospitals refused to give us the names and addresses of patients released during the last three months. Though there was no cost to them, they didn't want some strange foundation mucking about their privacy.

We finally ended up with sixty hospitals that were really representative of all types and areas. With the help of a large national survey company, we sent questionnaires to six thousand patients and two thousand family members and tallied the results. We paid for all that. Then we gathered the CEOs of all these hospitals down in New Orleans for a few days. Each one got a book that was about two feet by one foot and two inches thick. On each page was the question that was asked and then across the top of the page was THIS IS WHAT THE NATIONAL AVERAGE IS for the answers to this question. Next came THIS IS WHAT THE AVERAGE FOR YOUR AREA WAS, and THIS IS WHAT THE AVERAGE WAS FOR YOUR SPECIALTY TYPE (for example, a university hospital compared to any other kind of area university hospital). And at the bottom was THESE ARE THE ANSWERS FOR YOUR HOSPITAL. So you could compare your hospital with other hospitals of the same type, in your area and nationally. This was really the basis of determining best practice.

Every hospital got only its own answers. It didn't get the specific answers for any other hospital, but it got the answers for the norm for the other hospitals. We encountered a number of hospitals that were quite protective of their own information. But you need to have that kind of information, and we did it about as objectively and as well as it could be done. This survey process generated some modifications to the questionnaire, but not many were needed.

The questionnaires were based on the patient's perspective in eight areas of patient satisfaction, as noted in the book *Through the Patient's Eyes*, published in 1993. The book and the subsequent DVD brought about a great change in the United States. The DVD portrays real patients talking about their expectations. In one scene, a woman says, "I want to know exactly what they want to do to me. I want to know all about it. I want to know about how it affects me and what choices I have, and I want to know what the outcomes are apt to be. I don't want it to be 'Just go to the operating room and we'll tell you about it later.'"

In another scene, a man says, "Doctor, I don't want to hear about this. You know what you have to do, so do it. Don't worry me by asking me do I want this or that." They both appear to be quite reasonable people and they are patients, not actors. As you look at these questionnaires, you have to recognize that you are not talking about a single type of response. You are looking at people with different expectations, different fears and different reactions to fear.

[27]

Picker Institute

With the first survey a success, this question came up: Okay, this is useful—how do we keep doing it? The answer was that we would sell the surveys and generate enough income to fund the research and make the operation self-supporting. So in 1987 we created Picker Institute to administer the surveys and oversee the research needed to advance the concept of patient-centered care. Under the able leadership of Susan Edgman-Levitan and Tom Delbanco, the institute profited from the sales of the surveys.

While some hospitals were reluctant to pay for a Picker Survey, we discovered, to our surprise, that big corporations like the Ford Motor Company wanted to make sure that when they paid for hospital services for their employees, their employees would be treated well. They began to underwrite surveys, and the idea spread and was supported by various states and by hospitals.

I felt that we'd really succeeded when the hospitals began to be willing to have the results published. For example, almost all the hospitals in Massachusetts paid to be surveyed, having agreed that a year would go by during which they would try to improve their scores. At the end of that year, they'd have another Picker Survey. This time the results would be published in the newspapers. This proved that the healthcare profession was taking the surveys seriously.

Most states didn't, but California and a whole flock of big states followed Massachusetts's lead. At the same time, the U.S. Government was quite interested in using this tool to survey veterans' and other governmental hospitals, such as military hospitals.

The government couldn't afford to use a sole provider and wanted to use its own survey. We agreed to design a survey similar to ours in partnership with Harvard. A team from Picker Institute and Harvard produced what is known as a CAHPS (Consumer Assessment of Healthcare Providers and Systems) survey. Picker Institute didn't get the federal business, but on the other hand, the government now uses the kind of survey we promoted and knows how their people are being treated, be they military, administrative or veterans. The U.S. Government has stuck to that and has enlarged it.

As more and more hospitals asked the institute to survey their patient populations, Picker Institute wasn't able to handle the volume of business coming in. It became increasingly difficult to tabulate the responses by hand, as had been done initially, and while computers were advancing to the point where they could process the information quickly and accurately, the institute's attempts to computerize the process failed.

When we looked around for an established research organization that would be interested in taking over the survey component, Michael Hays of the National Research Corp. convinced us that he could handle the job. The institute sold the surveys to NRC in 2001, and NRC has done a very good job of administering the business. The surveys, designed to see hospital stays "through the patient's eyes," have become part of the fabric of medical services in this country.

With the sale of the survey business to NRC, Picker Institute turned its attention to advancing patient-centered care in other ways. Our talented board members Mark Waxman, Esq., Dr. Steve Schoenbaum, Sam Fleming, Dr. Sir Donald Irvine, Dr. David Leach and Gail Warden, working with Lucile O. Hanscom as executive director, developed a wide range of matching-grant programs, as well as the annual Picker Awards for Excellence® in the Advancement of Patient-Centered Care.

[28]
The Future of Healthcare in This Country

When I was teaching political science at Colgate, I had my own personal principle about democracy. It was: In a democracy, no matter how clearly you can see a catastrophe coming, you will not get change until the public finds the pain of the current conditions is greater than the perceived pain of changing them. As long as the American public thinks it is getting good medical treatment—despite clear evidence that it is not—the system won't change. And there's no way of changing it that I can see.

You and I get very, very good healthcare. We get it pretty close to when we want it. We get it where we want it, and our greatest troubles are minor ones. But if you go down to the hospitals in New York City that treat the indigent, you will see not only the indigent but the people who are well above indigent: a single mother, with no one to help her, who works all day and has two children at home whom she can't take to a doctor. She can't get time off and she has to feed the children, and you see the results in the mortality database.

This country, which spends huge amounts on an anti-missile system that will probably never work, could easily, for just a tiny part of that cost, provide healthcare for everybody. You could easily change the medical system as it operates now to reduce the money spent on administration and provide much more clinical care for every dollar you spend.

When we founded Picker Institute, we looked at various things we could do and settled on patient-centered care. When we started, we had no idea what kind of impact this could have, and we spent several years finding ways not to succeed. But we did pick something that was analogous, in size and scope, to what we had done in radiology, with the hope that the same thing would happen, that it would take off on its own and become so widespread that you wouldn't need us any more, as in radiology.

With regard to making patient-centered care part of a physician's education, we felt that it was very important to introduce the concept into medical school curricula. Working with the dean of the medical school at Harvard, Jean and I funded the creation of a course designed to change the curriculum of medical school—the "longitudinal introduction to clinical medicine." Instead of the standard medical school curriculum, which teaches abstract science for two years and then practice for two years, the course started out with entering students seeing patients and learning their sciences as part of learning how to treat those patients.

I attended one of the early classes. The doctor was explaining that the way to differentiate between a torn tendon in the foot and a muscle injury is to rotate the ankle. If the tendon is broken, there is no particular pain; if it is a muscle injury, there will be pain. When a student said, "I don't want to hurt the patient," the teacher politely asked the student if she had a better way of differentiating between these conditions, because each has to be treated differently.

I think that story indicates that people entering medical school have a natural tendency to be patient-centered. That inclination gets rubbed out of them in the current curriculum, which tends to focus on how you treat the disease technically. Yet you could just as well focus on being sure that the patient gets adequate anesthesia and is not hurt unduly, that the patient is adequately warned of what's happening and is given a chance to discuss it. Since medical schools are accredited, it would be possible for them to introduce patient-centered care into the system.

When I was on the federally mandated board of the National Fund for Medical Education, there was great concern over the cost of diagnostic testing and holding the cost of medicine down. One of the obvious targets is to try to reduce unnecessary diagnostic testing. We set up a program to teach medical school students that if they ran more diagnostic tests, they could probably find things they couldn't with one, or two or three. But they could do very well with four, and save a tremendous amount of money that would allow them to take care of more patients. These young students learned about the need to use only those diagnostic tests that were required.

We looked at the graduating students and saw that we had succeeded in convincing them that they could reduce the number of tests to only those that were necessary and get extremely good results. Unfortunately, when we decided to go back three years later, we found that the students were right back to ordering a flock of tests they didn't need.

Why? Because the doctors they were practicing with, the mentors they looked up to, still held to the culture of the old system. You need to watch very closely to make sure that what you teach students is what they actually practice, and not what their grandfathers did, or their mentors do.

Patient-centered care is now taken very seriously by the healthcare industry, the government, the payors, HMOs and insurance companies. It's become embedded in the culture.

In 2003 I received a Healthcare Quality Award from the National Committee for Quality Assurance. This was a recognition that patient-centered was a quality-assurance project, and that Picker had been the first organization to recognize its importance.

There's always more work to be done in the field of patient-centered care, but at some point I think we will reach the same stage as we did in radiology. Once the importance of academic radiology was recognized by the government, we didn't have to keep pushing it. We got out of the field because we weren't needed any more. And I think the time will certainly come, in the foreseeable future, that patient-centered care is so well recognized that it will continue on its own.

A Short Biography of Harvey Picker

Harvey Picker was born in New York City on Dec. 8, 1915. He graduated from the Fieldston School in Manhattan in 1932, from Colgate University in 1936 and from Harvard Business School with an MBA in 1938. During that time he also studied at Oxford University.

In 1938, Harvey joined Picker X-ray Company, which his father had founded two decades earlier, and served as president until 1970. He continued in that role after the company was sold to CIT in 1958.

Harvey joined the Navy as a provisional ensign in 1939, and his unit was called up in 1940. When he was invalided out of active duty in 1941, he was assigned to the Radiation Laboratory at MIT in Cambridge, Massachusetts.

After the war, Harvey headed Picker X-Ray Company for twenty-five years. In 1947 he married Jean Sovatkin, whom he had met in 1946. In 1963 President Lyndon Johnson appointed Jean the U.S. ambassador to the UN's Social and Economic Committee.

In the early 1950s, and as a result of his friendship with Herman Kahn and their mutual concern with the development and use of nuclear weapons, Harvey founded what was to become the Hudson Institute.

In 1971, Harvey returned to his alma mater, Colgate University, as an adjunct faculty member.

In 1972, he was asked to serve as dean of the Columbia University School of International and Public Affairs. He remained there until 1983, and the school tripled in size under his stewardship.

An avid sailor, Harvey bought Wayfarer Marine, one of the largest boatyards on the East Coast, in 1982. In 1983, he and Jean moved to Camden, Maine, where the yard was located.

Jean Picker died in 1990.

In 1994 Harvey took over the operations of Picker Institute, which he had founded at the suggestion of and in partnership with Jean in 1987. A global independent nonprofit organization, Picker Institute is dedicated to advancing the principles of patient-centered care as seen "through the patient's eyes." He continued to run the institute until his death.

Harvey died on March 22, 2008, at the age of 92. The last few months of his life were for family and friends, and this oral history was not at the top of the list of things he wanted to do. That is why the account of his life after he and Jean moved to Camden in 1983 is only a rough outline.

Branta *under full sail.*

CPSIA information can be obtained at www.ICGtesting.com
Printed in the USA
BVOW070937010612